THE
DOG LOVER'S GUIDE
TO LAKE TAHOE

Timbercreek Publishing

The Dog Lover's Guide To Lake Tahoe

By Susie Denison

Notice
This is intended as a guide to provide information and is not an endorsement
or recommendation by the author. No liability is assumed, with respect to
the accuracy and completeness of the information or from any loss or
injury incurred from the use of this book. All maps used in this book are
for reference only, they are not guaranteed to be accurate. Mileages used
in this book may vary.

Front Cover Photo: Steve Hall
Inside Photos: Susie Denison
Back Cover Photo: Kim Fiester
Maps: Lake Lizard Graphix

ISBN: 0-9664908-1-9
Library of Congress Catalog
Card Number: 2002109037

Printed in the United States of America.

"He is my other eyes that can see above the clouds;

My other ears that hear above the winds.

He is the part of me that can reach out into the sea.

He has told me a thousand times over that I am his reason for being;

By the way he rest against my leg;

By the way he thumps his tail at my smallest smile;

By the way he shows his hurt when I leave without taking him.

When I am wrong, he is delighted to forgive.

When I am angry, he clowns to make me smile.

When I am happy, he is joy unbounded.

When I am a fool, he ignores it.

When I succeed, he brags.

Without him, I am only another man.

With him, I am all-powerful.

He is loyalty itself.

He has taught me the meaning of devotion.

With him, I know a secret comfort and a private peace.

He has brought me understanding where before I was ignorant.

His head on my knee can heal my human hurts.

His presence by my side is protection against my fears of dark and unknown things.

He has promised to wait for me... whenever... wherever - in case I need him.

And I expect I will - as I always have. He is my dog."

-- Gene Hill

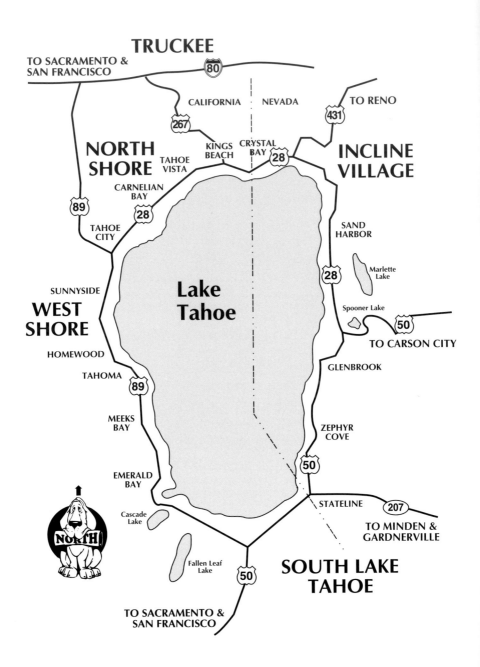

TABLE OF CONTENTS

Cross Country Skiing

Sledding Hills

Swimming Areas

Fishing Spots

Other Doggie Adventures

Dog Services

IMPORTANT PHONE NUMBERS

Animal Shelters
•Truckee Animal Shelter (530) 582-7830
•Placer County Animal Shelter (530) 546-4269
•El Dorado County Animal Shelter, SLK Tahoe (530) 577-1766
•Wildlife Rescue, North Lake Tahoe (530) 546-1211
•Lake Tahoe Wildlife Care, SLK Tahoe (530) 577-2273
•Pet Network of North Lake Tahoe (775) 832-4404
•Humane Society of Truckee (530) 587-5948
•South Lake Tahoe Humane Society (530) 577-4521

Emergency Numbers
•Animal Poison Control (800) 548-2423
•Donner-Truckee Vet Emergency Services (530) 587-4366
•North Lake Vet Emergency Services (530) 583-8587
•Incline Vet Emergency Services (775) 831-0433
•South Tahoe Vet Emergency Services (530) 541-3551

🐾 = Very Dog-Friendly

He is your friend, your partner,
Your defender, your dog.
You are his life, his love, his leader.
He will be yours, faithful and true,
To the last beat of his heart.
You owe it to him to be worthy
of such devotion.

–Unknown

LODGING

Buddy, Weimeriner

TRUCKEE

Alpine Country Lodge
Walk to Donner Lake. Rates are $60 to $105 a night, and $10 per dog.
11260 Deer Field Drive, Truckee (530) 587-3801 or (800) 933-1787
Website: www.alpinecountrylodge.com

Inn at Truckee
More than 1 dog ok but dogs cannot be left unattended in room.
Hot tub, sauna, free continental breakfast. Rates are $69 to $133 a night,
and $11 per night for a dog.
11506 Deer Field Drive, Truckee (530) 587-8888 or (888) 773-6888
Website: www.innattruckee.com

Sunset Inn
Located in downtown Truckee near the high school. Rates are $45 to $55
a night, dogs stay free. 11700 Donner Pass Road, Truckee (530) 587-8234

NORTH SHORE

Hauserman Rental Group 🐾
The Hauserman Rental Group has cabins and houses for you and your dog to
stay in. No more having to worry about where to leave your dog when you go
skiing. Choose from rustic cabins to lakefront homes. The rentals that allow
dogs go quickly, so make your reservations early. Check out their website,
where you can find pictures, rates and descriptions of all their vacation
homes. Rates are $75 to $400 a night, with a $15 extra cleaning fee for dogs.
475 North Lake Blvd, Tahoe City (530) 583-3793 or (800) 20-TAHOE
Website: www.enjoytahoe.com
E-mail: rentals@enjoytahoe.com

Beesley's Cottages

Located on 3 acres of lakefront property with 300 feet of sandy beach. There are 8 lakefront cottages, most with fireplaces and kitchens. Dogs are greeted with a scarf and a dog bowl filled with biscuits and are allowed leash-free. Open Memorial Day thru Nov. 1, closed for the winter. Rates are $80 to $160 a night, dogs stay free. 6674 North Lake Blvd, Tahoe Vista (530) 546-2448

Falcon Lodge

Lakefront rooms available. Private sandy beach that allows dogs. Indoor spa and large heated swimming pool open in summer. Rates are $49 to $179 a night, and $10 per dog per night.
8258 North Lake Blvd, Kings Beach (530) 546-2583 or (800) 682-4631

Holiday House

These lakefront rooms share a large deck with a panoramic view of Lake Tahoe. BBQ, hot tub, and boat buoy available. Rates are $85 to $125 a night, with a $25 dog fee.
7276 North Lake Blvd, Tahoe Vista (530) 546-2369

North Lake Lodge

Choose from a room or private cabin, some with kitchens. Hot tub, walk to the lake. Rates are $75 to $100, and $5 per dog per night. There is a 20% discount during the off-seasons.
8716 North Lake Blvd, Kings Beach (530) 546-2731 or (888) 923-5253
Website: www.tahoeguide.com/go/northlakelodge
E-mail: nlklodge@sierra.net

Roo, Australian Healer/Husky mix

North Shore Lodge

Your choice of a cabin or a room. There is a fenced in BBQ area to let your dog run. Swimming pool open during summer. Rates are $50 to $200 a night, and $10 per dog per night.
8755 North Lake Blvd, Kings Beach (530) 546-4833
E-mail: nshorlodge@powernet.net

Rustic Cottages

These cozy cabins have all been upgraded. Complimentary continental breakfast and free video rental. Rates are $59 to $149 a night, and $10 per dog per night.
7499 North Lake Blvd, Tahoe Vista (530) 546-3523 or (888) 778-7842
Website: www.rusticcottages.com
E-mail: rustic@rusticcottages.com

Stevenson's Inn
Just follow the path to the lake! Hot tub and swimming pool open during summer. No leaving pets alone in your room. More than one dog welcome. Rates are $69 to $129 a night, and $5 per dog per night.
8742 North Lake Blvd, Kings Beach (530) 546-2269 or (800) 634-9141
Website: www.stevensonsinn.qpg.com
E-mail: laketahoes@aol.com

Tahoe Luxury Properties
Focusing on luxury rentals from a 1 bedroom lakefront and up. Rates are $150 to $1000 a night, and there is no extra fee for dogs.
(530) 583-8823 or (800) 581-8828
Website: www.tluxp.com
E-mail: kelly@tluxp.com

Tahoe Moon Properties 🐾
They have everything from small cabins to luxury homes that sleep 30 people and almost all of them are dog-friendly. Rates are $200 to $600 a night, and $30 per dog per stay. (530) 581-2771 or (866) 581-2771
Website: www.tahoemoonproperties.com
E-mail: info@tahoemoonrentals.com

Three Buck Inn 🐾
Located just across from the Truckee River, this new hotel is beautifully decorated and is very dog friendly! Dogs are greeted with dog cookies, a dog bed and a water bowl for their stay. There is also a community dog shower with shampoo and towels provided. You can follow a hiking trail right out the door, where your dog can run leash free and swim in the river. Rates are $125 to $350 a night, and dogs stay free.
P.O. Box 2048, Olympic Valley (530) 550-8600
Website: www.threebuckinn.com
E-mail: threebuckinn@juno.com

Woodvista Lodge
More than 1 dog welcome. Hot tub open all year, pool open in summer. Rates are $55 to $130 a night, and $10 per dog per night.
7699 North Lake Blvd, Tahoe Vista (530) 546-3839

WEST SHORE

Norfolk Woods Inn
These cozy cabins have 2 bedrooms upstairs and a full kitchen downstairs. Rates are $150 to $190 a night, and $10 per dog per night.
6941 West Lake Blvd, Tahoma (530) 525-5000
Website: www.norfolkwoods.com   E-mail: norfwds@sierra.net

Tahoe Lake Cottages
Your choice of a 1 or 2 bedroom cabin with a full kitchen. Pool, hot tub and BBQ area. Rates are $130 to $265 a night, and $10 per dog per night.
7030 West Lake Blvd, Tahoma (530) 525-4411 or (800) 852-8246
Website: www.tahoelakecottages.com
E-mail: mike@tahoelakecottages.com

Tahoma Lodge
These cabins have a full kitchen and a woodstove or fireplace. Pool, jacuzzi and access to a private beach. Rates are $65 to $275 a night, dogs stay free.
7018 West Lake Blvd, Tahoma (530) 525-7721
Website: www.tahomalodge.com
E-mail: info@tahomalodge.com

Tahoma Meadows B & B Cottages
Nicely decorated cottages, some with fireplaces. Rates are $95 to $295 a night and there is a $25 cleaning fee for dogs.
PO Box 810, Homewood (530) 525-9990
Website: www.tahomameadows.com
E-mail: info@tahomameadows.com

West Lake Properties
Vacation rental houses and cabins on the north and west shores. Rates are $125 to $300 a night, dogs stay free.
115 West Lake Blvd, Tahoe City (530) 583-0268 or (800) 870-8201
Website: www.westlakeproperties.com
E-mail: info@westlakeproperties.com

INCLINE VILLAGE

Coldwell Banker Incline Realty Inc.
Vacation rental houses and condos. There are only a few that allow dogs, so make your reservations early. Rates are $130 to $225 a night.
795 Mays Blvd, Incline Village (775) 831-4800 or (800) 572-5009
Website: www.2ctahoe.com/incline
E-mail: cbrentals@aol.com

Lucy, Australian Sheppard

SOUTH LAKE TAHOE

Alder Inn

Close to Heavenly Ski Resort. Swimming pool and hot tub. Rates are $39 to $105 a night, and $12 per dog per night.
1072 Ski Run Bl, SLK Tahoe (530) 544-4485 or (800) 544-0056
Website: www.alderinn.com

Blue Jay Lodge

Some of these rooms have fireplaces and kitchens. Swimming pool and hot tub. Rates are $39 to $99, and $10 per dog per night.
4133 Cedar Ave, SLK Tahoe (530) 544-5232 or (800) 258-3529
Website: www.bluejaylodge.com

Cedar Lodge

There are limited rooms that allow dogs. Located 1 block from casinos and 2 blocks from the lake. Hot Tub. Rates are $40 to $80 a night, with a $10 fee and a $40 refundable deposit for dogs.
4081 Cedar Ave, SLK Tahoe (530) 541-5004 or (800) 222-1177
Website: www.cedarlodgetahoe.com

Coldwell Banker McKinney & Associates

Vacation rental houses and cabins. There are only a few that allow dogs, so make your reservations early. Rates are $125 to $250 a night, dogs stay free.
2196 Lake Tahoe Blvd, SLK Tahoe (530) 542-0557 or (800) 748-6857
Website: www.stayintahoe.com E-mail: stayintahoe@tahoesnow.com

Days Inn- Stateline South Lake Tahoe

There are limited rooms that allow dogs. Dogs cannot be left alone in room late at night or early in the morning. Dogs are not allowed over holidays. Rates are $42 to $114 a night, and $5 per dog per night. 3 dog maximum per room. 968 Park Ave, SLK Tahoe (530) 541-4800 or (800) 325-2525
Website: www.daysinncasinoarea.com E-mail: dayscasino@aol.com

Harrah's Tahoe

Dogs are not allowed in the rooms, but Rover can stay in one of Harrah's 5 kennels, for $10 per night. There are grassy areas outside, and the beach is just a 10 minute walk. Along with a swimming pool and 2 hot tubs, Harrah's has a health club and 6 restaurants. Rates are $99 to $200 a night. Hwy 50, Stateline (775) 588 6611 or (800) 427-7247

Holly's Place for Women

Holly's place is for all women. They are gay and straight friendly. Choose from a cabin or a room. The resort is fully fenced in- so dogs can stretch their legs. A portion of the proceeds are donated to various women's charities. Rates are $130 to $395 a night, and $15 per dog per day. There is a $100 refundable security deposit. (530) 544-7040 or (800) 745-7041
Website: www.hollysplace.com
E-mail: cphillips@hollysplace.com

Inn at Heavenly

Rooms with fireplaces and kitchenettes. Free continental breakfast, spa room. Rates are $89 to $175 a night, and $20 per dog per night. 1261 Ski Run Blvd, SLK Tahoe (530) 544-4244 or (800) MY-CABIN
Website: www.800mycabin.com
E-mail: mycabin@sierra.net

Lake Tahoe Accommodations

Choose from a wide selection of rental homes, mostly located near Heavenly Valley. Rates are $88 to $145 a night.
2048 Dunlap Drive, SLK Tahoe (530) 544-3234 or (800) 544-3234

Lake Tahoe Inn

Dogs cannot be left alone in room. These rooms are located 1 block from the casinos. Complimentary breakfast. Swimming pool and hot tub. Rates are $69 to $135 a night. Dogs require a $100 deposit.
4110 Lake Tahoe Bl, SLK Tahoe (530) 541-2010 or (800) 972-8557
Website: www.laketahoeinn.com
E-mail: laketinn@aol.com

Lake Tahoe Lodging
Vacation rental cabins, condos and homes in South Lake Tahoe. Rates are $125 to $600 a night, and a $75 non-refundable pet fee.
292 Kingsbury Grade, Stateline (775) 588-5253 or (800) 654-5253
Website: www.laketahoelodging.com
E-mail: marni@laketahoelodging.com

Lake Village Resort
Several of their vacation rental condos are pet-friendly. Rates range from $150 - $300 a night and $20 per dog per night.
301 Highway 50, Zephyr Cove (775) 589-6065

Lampliter Inn
This bed and breakfast is located 1 block from the casinos. Hot tub. Rates are $44 to $104 a night and $10 per dog per night.
4143 Cedar Ave, SLK Tahoe (530) 544-2936 or (888) 544-4055
Website: www.lampliterinn.com
E-mail: lampliter@msn.com

Matterhorn Motel
Some rooms have kitchens and fireplaces. Heated swimming pool, hot tub. Dogs cannot be left unattended in room. Rates are $30 to $200 a night and $10 per dog per night.
2187 Lake Tahoe Blvd, SLK Tahoe (530) 541-0367
E-mail: matmotel@aol.com

Motel 6
One small dog per room allowed. Swimming pool. Rates are $39 to $59 a night, dogs stay free.
2375 Lake Tahoe Bl, SLK Tahoe (530) 542-1400 or (800) 4-Motel-6
Website: www.motel6.com

Sandor's Chateau Motel

This motel is situated in a park-like setting on an acre at the edge of town. Rates are $75 to $135 a night and dogs stay free.
1137 Emerald Bay Road, SLK Tahoe (530) 541-6312 or (877) SANDORS

Sorensen's Resort

This resort offers 6 dog-friendly cabins, all with kitchens and some with fireplaces. It is located on 165 acres, where your dog can run leash-free. There is a full service restaurant on-site. The resort offers educational programs for both adults and kids, including history tours, birdwatching, snowshoing, medicine in the mountains and many others. There is dog-friendly cross country skiing nearby. Located in Hope Valley, which is about 20 miles south of Lake Tahoe and 15 miles from Kirkwood Ski Resort. Rates are $115 to $395 a night, dogs stay free.
14255 Hwy 88, Hope Valley (530) 694-2203 or (800) 423-9949
Website: www.sorensensresort.com
E-mail: sorensensresort@yahoo.com

Spruce Grove Cabins & Cottages

There are 7 cabins, all 1 & 2 bedrooms with full kitchens and fireplaces. Hot tub. Close to Heavenly. Rates are $150 to $195 a night and $10 per dog per night.
3599 Spruce St, SLK Tahoe, (530) 544-0549 or (800) 777-0914
Website: www.sprucegrovetahoe.com
E-mail: info@sprucegrovetahoe.com

Super 8 Motel

This motel has a nice large grassy lawn out front where you can walk your dog. There is also a restaurant with outdoor picnic tables where your pooch can join you for a bite to eat. Rates are $40 to $160 a night and $10 per dog per day.
3600 Lake Tahoe Blvd, SLK Tahoe, (530) 544-3476 or (800) 237-8882

Stovall's Tahoe Inn

There are limited rooms that allow dogs. All rooms have gas fireplaces, microwaves and refrigerators. Swimming pool and hot tub. Rates are $59 to $99 a night, with a $20 dog fee.
4075 Manzanita Ave, SLK Tahoe (530) 544-2285 or (800) 659-4185
Website: www.stovallinn.com
E-mail: seller527@hotmail.com

Tahoe Colony Inn 🐾

Dogs cannot be left alone in rooms. Swimming pool and hot tub open year round. Rates are $48 to $110 a night, dogs stay free with a refundable $40 deposit. 3794 Montreal Rd, SLK Tahoe (530) 544-6481 or (800) 338-5552
Website: www.americana-inns.com or www.gototahoe.com
E-mail: tahoecol@sierra.net

Tahoe Cottage Inn

Choose from a room or a cabin with a kitchens. Rates are $40 to $80 a night, dogs stay free.
1220 Emerald Bay Rd, SLK Tahoe (530) 541-3411

Tahoe Keys Resort

Waterfront condos and homes available, but only some allow dogs. Rates vary depending on home.
599 Tahoe Keys Blvd, SLK Tahoe, (530) 544-5397 or (800) 698-2463
Website: www.tahoevacationguide.com
E-mail: info@tahoevacationguide.com

Tahoe Sundowner Motel

There are limited rooms that allow dogs. Located near the 'Y'. Hot tub. Rates are $30 to $150 a night and $5 per dog per night.
1211 Emerald Bay Road, SLK Tahoe, (530) 541-2282 or (800) 246-5556

Tahoe Tropicana Lodge

There are limited rooms that allow dogs. Located 1 block from the casinos.
Some rooms have kitchens. Swimming pool, hot tub. Rates are $30 to $95 a
night and $5 per dog per night.
4132 Cedar Ave, SLK Tahoe, (530) 541-3911 or (800) 447-0246
Website: www.tahoetroplcana.com
E-mail: trop60@cs.com

Tahoe Valley Lodge

There are limited rooms that allow small dogs. Only 1 dog per room. Dogs
cannot be left in rooms alone. All rooms have gas fireplaces. Swimming
pool, hot tub. Rates are $95 to $175 a night, $5 per dog per night.
2241 Lake Tahoe Bl, SLK Tahoe (530) 541-0353
Website: www.tahoevalleylodge.com
E-mail: ed@tahoevalleylodge.com

Zephyr Cove Resort

Walking distance to the lake! Dogs are allowed in some of the cabins, but
not in the lodge. Rates are $100 to $315 a night, and $10 per dog per night.
460 Highway 50, Zephyr Cove (775) 588-6644
Website: www.zephyrcove.com
E-mail: zcr-lodge@aramark.com

I know love. I had a dog.

–Beth Brown

CAMPGROUNDS

German Shepherd

TRUCKEE

Cottonwood Campground

Located along Cottonwood Creek, this private campsite is fairly secluded from the highway. Enjoy fishing and hiking. Dogs must be leashed. Closed for the winter. 49 sites, $9 fee. From Truckee, drive north on Hwy 89 for 19.5 miles. Look for the sign on the side of the highway. For more information, call (800) 280-CAMP.

Donner Memorial State Park

This campsite offers many recreational activities, including fishing, swimming, rafting, canoeing, hiking, nature walks, and watercraft rentals. There is a lagoon and Donner Lake to explore. Dogs must be leashed. Closed for the winter. 154 sites, $12 to $16 fee and $1 per dog per day. From Truckee, drive west 3 miles on Donner Pass Road. For more information, call (800) 444-PARK.

Logger Campground

This large, well maintained campsite has paved roads and a nearby public boat ramp. Enjoy fishing and boating on the Stampede Reservoir. Dogs must be leashed. Closed for the winter. 252 sites, $11 fee. From Truckee, drive 7 miles east on I-80 and take the Hirschdale Exit. Turn on the Boca-Stampede Road, and drive north for 8 miles to the campsite. For more information, call (800) 280-CAMP.

Martis Creek Campground

This secluded campground is well maintained and has private, well-spaced sites. There is hiking, mountain biking, and fly fishing nearby. The campground is located near the Truckee-Tahoe Airport, so there may be some noise. Dogs must be leashed. Closed for the winter. 25 sites, $10 fee. From Truckee, drive south on Hwy 267 for 5 miles and turn left at the Martis Creek sign. For more information, call (530) 639-2342.

Goose Meadows Campground

This campsite is right on the Truckee River. It is also right on Hwy 89. There is traffic noise, and not much privacy, but the fishing is great! Dogs must be leashed. Closed for the winter. 27 sites, $8 fee. Located approximately 9 miles north of Tahoe City on Hwy 89. For more information, call (800) 280-CAMP.

Granite Flat Campground

Located just south of Truckee, on Hwy 89, this riverfront campground is a great spot for fishing. Dogs must be leashed. Closed for the winter. 72 sites, $12 fee. Located 3/4 of a mile south of Truckee on Hwy 89. For more information, call (800) 280-CAMP.

NORTH SHORE

Lake Forest Campground

This campground, located just outside Tahoe City, has a boat ramp, a pier, and a small rocky beach for your dog to swim. Dogs must be leashed. Closed for the winter. 20 sites, $12 fee. From Tahoe City, drive east on Hwy 28 for 2 miles. Turn right on Lake Forest Road, and right into the campground. For more information, call (530) 583-5544.

Sandy Beach Campground

Located in Tahoe Vista, this campsite has easy access to the lake. Dogs must be leashed. Closed for the winter. 44 sites, $15 to $20 fee. Located at 6873 North Lake Blvd, Tahoe Vista. For more information, call (530) 546-7682.

Silver Creek Campground

Located on the Truckee River, this campsite is very close to Hwy 89. You and your dog can hike up Deer Creek, or fish in the Truckee River. This campground is just south of Goose Meadows. Dogs must be leashed. Closed for the winter. 31 sites, $8 fee. Located approximately 6 miles north of Tahoe City on Hwy 89, near Squaw Valley. For more information, call (800) 280-CAMP.

Tahoe State Recreation Area

This lakefront campground is right in Tahoe City. It's in walking distance to shops, restaurants and is right next to the bike path. It's also right on the main road, so it may be noisy. Dogs must be leashed. Closed for the winter. 31 sites, $16 fee, dogs are $1 a day. Located just east of the Safeway Shopping Center, on Hwy 28 in Tahoe City. For more information, call (800) 444-PARK.

WEST SHORE

General Creek Campground

One of just a few campsites open over winter. Located at Sugar Pine Point State Park which is near the lake, bike path and hiking trails. Dogs must be leashed and are only allowed in the campground and on paved roads. Open all year. 175 sites, $16 fee. From Tahoe City, drive south 9 miles on Hwy 89 to General Creek Campground and Sugar Pine Point State Park. For more information, call (800) 444-PARK.

Kaspian Campground

This small campsite in Blackwood Canyon is close to the lake and bike path. There can be highway noise. Dogs must be leashed. Closed for the winter. 10 sites, $10 fee. From Tahoe City, drive 5 miles south on Hwy 89. For more information, call (800) 280-CAMP.

Meeks Bay Campground

Located close to Hwy 89, this campsite has little privacy and can be noisy. It does, however have a private sandy beach and boat ramp. Dogs must be leashed. Closed for the winter. 40 sites, $14 fee. For more information, call (800) 280-CAMP.

William Kent Campground

Situated close to the lake, bike path, and Sunnyside Lodge, this campsite has plenty to keep you busy. Dogs must be leashed. Closed for the winter. 95 sites, $12 fee. From Tahoe City, drive 2 miles south on Hwy 89 and look for the signs. For more information, call (800) 280-CAMP.

INCLINE VILLAGE

Mount Rose Campground

This campsite is in the Toiyabe National Forest, and is surrounded by great hiking trails. Dogs must be leashed. Closed for the winter. 24 sites, $8 fee. Drive north on Hwy 431 (Mount Rose Hwy) for 9 miles. The campsite is on your right. For more information, call (800) 280-CAMP.

SOUTH LAKE TAHOE

Emerald Bay Boat-In Camp

One of the most popular campsites around, this spot is complete with a large pier and a long sandy beach. Check out Vikingsholm during the day, and camp here at night. Dogs must be leashed and are not allowed in Vikingsholm. Closed for the winter. 20 sites, $10 fee. Located on the north side of Emerald Bay. For more information, call (530) 525-7277.

Emerald Bay State Park

Secluded from the highway, this large campground has wonderful views of the lake. There is a 1/4 mile hike to the Emerald Bay Beach from most sites. This is a very popular spot. Dogs must be leashed, and are only allowed in the campground and on paved roads. Closed for the winter. 100 sites, $16 fee. For more information, call (800) 444-PARK.

Fallen Leaf Lake Campground

This private and secluded campsite offers swimming, hiking, fishing, biking and boating. Dogs must be leashed. Closed for the winter. 205 sites, $14 fee. From South Lake Tahoe Y, drive 2 miles north on Hwy 89 to Fallen Leaf Lake Road. For more information, call (800) 280-CAMP.

KOA of South Lake Tahoe

This campsite right off Hwy 50 has a swimming pool, a small market, and is near the Upper Truckee River. Dogs must be leashed. Closed for the winter. 60 sites, $23 to $29 fee. Dogs are an extra $3.50 per dog per day. From South Lake Tahoe Y, drive south on Hwy 50 for 4.6 miles, the campground will be on your left. For more information, call (530) 577-3693.

Nevada Beach & Campground

This campsite is next to a sandy beach on the shore of Lake Tahoe. Enjoy swimming, boating, and volleyball. The beach may be packed with people during the day. Dogs must be leashed. Closed for the winter. 54 sites, $16 fee. From South Lake Tahoe, drive east on Hwy 50, 1 mile past Stateline Nevada to Elks Point Road. For more information, call (800) 280-CAMP.

South Lake Tahoe Recreation Area

Located just off Hwy 50, this campsite is nicely maintained and offers access to a nearby pool and fitness center. Enjoy swimming and boating in the lake. This is a great spot for RVs. Dogs must be leashed. Closed for the winter. 160 sites, $16.50 fee, plus $1 per dog per day. From South Lake Tahoe Y, drive east on Hwy 50 for 2.5 miles to Rufus Allen Blvd. Follow the signs to the campsite. For more information, call (530) 542-6096.

Tahoe Pines Campground

This campsite is located right next to the KOA Campground. It is right on the Upper Truckee River, and offers a small beach with places to swim. Dogs must be leashed. Closed for the winter. 80 sites, $22 to $29 fee. Dogs are an extra $3.50 per dog per day. From South Lake Tahoe Y, drive south on Hwy 50 for 4.5 miles. The campground is on the left. For more information, call (530) 577-1653.

Tahoe Valley Campground

Just off the main road, this large, clean campsite is a great family spot. Enjoy a swimming pool, tennis courts and the Upper Truckee River, which runs through the campsite. Dogs must be leashed. Closed for the winter. 412 sites, $20 to $29 fee. From South Lake Tahoe Y, drive south on Hwy 50 for 1/2 mile. Turn left on C St. and follow the signs to the campsite. For more information, call (530) 541-2222.

Zephyr Cove Campground

There's not much privacy at this campsite on the beach. This is a very popular beach spot during the summer. Enjoy swimming, volleyball and boating. Dogs must be leashed. Open all year. 170 sites, $17 to $24 fee. From South Lake Tahoe, drive northeast on Hwy 50, 14 miles past Stateline, Nevada to Zephyr Cove. Follow the signs to the campsite. For more information, call (775) 588-6644.

Dogs are not our whole life,
but they make our lives whole.

-Roger Caras

RESTAURANTS

Inga, Bernese Mountain Dog

TRUCKEE

Ames Deli Mart

Deli sandwiches. Sit at an outside table with your dog.

12716 Northwoods, Truckee (530) 587-1717

Dairy Queen 🐾

Hamburgers, ice cream. Eat at a table outside, and get a free 'puppy cup' of vanilla ice cream for your dog.

11355 Donner Pass Road, Donner Plaza, Truckee (530) 587-7055

Earthly Delights

Pastries, cakes, sandwiches, salads. Dine with your doggie at the outside tables. 10087 West River St, Truckee (530) 587-7793

Gateway Deli

Deli sandwiches. Sit with your pooch at an outside table.

11012 Donner Pass Road, Truckee (530) 587-3106

Port of Subs

Sandwiches, salads. Eat at a table outside with your dog.

11260 Donner Pass Road, Truckee (530) 582-8060

Sizzler

Steak, seafood, salad. Your pooch can join you at a picnic table outside.

11262 Donner Pass Road, Truckee (530) 587-1824

Starbucks Coffee

Coffee, muffins, scones. Have a coffee and a snack with your dog at a table outside. 11260 Donner Pass Road, Truckee (530) 582-6856

Wild Cherries

Sandwiches, soup, salads. Grab a bite to eat at a table outside, and your dog will get a dog biscuit. 11429 Donner Pass Rd, Truckee (530) 582-5602

NORTH SHORE

Brockway Bakery

Sandwiches, ice cream, espresso. Eat with your dog at one of the outside tables. 8710 North Lake Blvd, Kings Beach (530) 546-2431

CB's Pizza & Grill

Pizza, sandwiches, salads. Sit with your dog at an outside table. 5075 North Lake Blvd, Carnelian Bay (530) 546-4738

The Char Pit

Burgers, sandwiches, tacos. Dine on the outside patio with your pooch. 8732 North Lake Blvd, Kings Beach (530) 546-3171

The Coffee Connection

Coffee, bagels, sandwiches. Dogs must be leashed or under the outdoor table. 950 North Lake Blvd, Tahoe City (530) 583-0725

Coyotes Mexican Cuisine

Tacos, burritos, mexican salads. There's lots of outdoor seating for you and your dog. 521 North Lake Blvd, Tahoe City (530) 583-6653

Dam Cafe

Espresso, smoothies, sandwiches, ice cream. You and your dog can eat at one of the tables outside. 55 West Lake Blvd, Tahoe City (530) 581-0278

Fiamma Cucina Rustica
Pizza, pasta, sandwiches. Enjoy this delicious cuisine at one of the outdoor tables. 521 North Lake Blvd, Tahoe City (530) 581-1416

The Java Hut
Coffee, pastries, bagel sandwiches. Have a coffee or snack at an outside table with your pooch.
8268 North lake Blvd, Kings Beach (530) 546-0602

Buddy, Golden Retriever

Naughty Dawg 🐾

Burgers, steaks, sandwiches. Dogs get a bowl of water when they eat with you on the patio.
255 North Lake Blvd, Tahoe City (530) 581-DAWG

Old Post Office Coffee Shop

Breakfast, burgers, salads. Well-behaved and leashed dogs may dine on the outside patio with their owners.
5245 North Lake Blvd, Carnelian Bay (530) 546-3205

Rosie's Cafe

Seafood, ribs, steak. Dine with your doggie at an outdoor table.
561 North Lake Blvd, Tahoe City (530) 583-8504

Sierra Vista Lakefront Dining

International Cuisine. Dine with your doggie outside, and enjoy the panoramic lakeviews. 700 North Lake Blvd, Tahoe City (530) 583-0233

Subway

Sandwiches, salads. Eat an an outside table with your dog.
8700 North Lake Blvd, Kings Beach (530) 546-8258

Syd's Bagelery and Expresso

Coffee, bagel sandwiches. Sit at a table outside with your dog.
550 North Lake Blvd, Tahoe City (530) 583-2666

Toni's Cafe

Burgers, salads, ice cream. Enjoy your lunch at an outside table with your dog. Open only in the summer.
8421 North Lake Blvd, Kings Beach (530) 546-2715

Nellie, Springer Spaniel

WEST SHORE

Black Bear Tavern

Pizza, pasta, steak, seafood. Eat at one of the tables on the outdoor deck with your dog. 2255 West Lake Blvd, Sunnyside (530) 583-8626

Obexer's Country Market

Deli sandwiches. Eat at a picnic table outside with your dog.
5300 West Lake Blvd, Homewood (530) 525-1300

Pisanos Pizza

Pizza, salads. Eat at one of the outdoor tables with your dog.
5335 West Lake Blvd, Homewood (530) 525-6464

Sunnyside Market

Deli and market. Have your lunch at an outside table with your dog.
1780 West Lake Blvd, Sunnyside (530) 583-7626

Tahoe House & Backerei

Homemade soups, sandwiches, baked goods. Dine with your doggie on
the outside patio. 625 West Lake Blvd, Tahoe City (530) 583-1377

West Shore Cafe

California Cuisine. Dine on the deck with your doggie. Open only in the
summer. 5180 West Lake Blvd, Homewood (530) 525-5200

INCLINE VILLAGE

Grog & Grist Market and Deli

Deli sandwiches. Sit with your dog at a table outside.
800 Tahoe Blvd, Incline Village (775) 831-1123

Hamburger Delite

Burgers, hot dogs, fries. Eat at one of the tables outside with your dog.
868 Tahoe Blvd, Incline Village (775) 832-2121

T's Mesquite Rotisserie

Sandwiches, burritos, salads. Dine with your doggie at a table outside.
901 Tahoe Blvd, Incline Village (775) 831-2832

Subway

Sandwiches, salads. Sit at a table outside with your dog.

317 Village Blvd, Incline Village (775) 831-3370

The Wildflower Cafe

Sandwiches, salads. Dine on the patio, while your dog hangs out in the fenced in area nearby. 869 Tahoe Blvd, Incline Village (775) 831-8072

SOUTH LAKE TAHOE

Bountiful Cafe

Breakfast, lunch. Eat at an outdoor table with your pooch.

717 Emerald Bay Road, SLK Tahoe (530) 542-4060

Carina's Cafe

Sandwiches, soups, salads. Dine at an outdoor table with your dog near the shore of Lake Tahoe. 3469 Lake Tahoe Blvd, SLK Tahoe (530) 541-3354

Chris' Cafe

Burgers, sandwiches. Sit outside at a table with your dog.

3140 Hwy 50, Meyers (530) 577-5132

Colombo's Burgers A-Go-Go

Burgers, fish & chips, chicken strips. Eat at an outdoor table with your pooch. 841 Emerald Bay Road, SLK Tahoe (530) 541-4646

Dixon's Restaurant & Brewery

Pasta, burgers, chicken, beer. Dine with your doggie at a table outside.

675 Emerald Bay Road, SLK Tahoe (530) 542-3389

Grass Roots Natural Foods
Natural foods. Eat with your dog at an outside table.
2040 Dunlap Drive, SLK Tahoe (530) 541-7788

Izzy's Burger Spa
Burgers, fries, shakes. Share a table outside with your dog.
2591 Hwy 50, SLK Tahoe (530) 544-5030

J&J Pizza
Pizza, calzones, salads. Sit at a table outside with your pooch.
2660 Lake Tahoe Blvd, SLK Tahoe (530) 542-2780

Kentucky Fried Chicken
Chicken, sandwiches. Sit at a table outside with your dog.
2136 Lake Tahoe Blvd, SLK Tahoe (530) 541-2727

Marie Callender's
Burgers, sandwiches, pies. Eat at a table outside with your dog.
3599 Lake tahoe Blvd, SLK Tahoe (530) 544-5535

Tucker and Buddy - Golden Retrievers
Zoey - Black Lab

Meyers Downtown Cafe

Breakfast, lunch. Eat at a table outside with your dog.
3200 Hwy 50, Meyers (530) 573-0228

Rude Brothers Bagel & Coffee Haus

Coffee, bagels, cookies, cinnamon rolls. Have a coffee or a snack at a table outside with your dog. 3117 Harrison Ave, SLK Tahoe (530) 541-8195

St. Bernard

Shoreline Cafe
Burgers, steaks, salads. Dogs are allowed at the outside tables overlooking Lake tahoe. 3310 Lake tahoe Blvd, SLK Tahoe (530) 541-7858

Sidestreet Cafe
Bagels, sandwiches, baked goods. Dine with your doggie at a table outside. 3988 Lake Tahoe Blvd, SLK Tahoe (530) 544-5393

Snow Flake Drive In
Burgers, fries. Sit at a table outside with your dog. 3057 Lake Tahoe Blvd, SLK Tahoe (530) 544-6377

Sprouts
Organic health foods, pasta, soup, sandwiches. Dine at a picnic table with your dog. 3125 Harrison Ave, SLK Tahoe (530) 541-6969

Subway
Sandwiches, salads. Eat at a table outside with your dog. 3924 Lake Tahoe Blvd, SLK Tahoe (530) 541-4334

Taco Bell
Tacos, burritos. Sit with your pooch at an outside table. 4109 Lake Tahoe Blvd, SLK Tahoe (530) 541-5233

Tahoe Keys Delicatessen
Deli sandwiches. Dine with your doggie at a table outside. 2301 Hwy 50, SLK Tahoe (530) 544-1335

Yellow Submarine
Sandwiches, salads. Sit at an outside table with your dog. Tallac Ave & Hwy 50, SLK Tahoe (530) 541-8808

The more I see of men, the more I like dogs.

-Madame Roland

DOG PARKS

Roxanne, Black Lab

TRUCKEE

Donner Memorial State Park
This state park offers many recreational activities, including camping, fishing, swimming, rafting, canoeing, hiking, nature walks, and watercraft rentals. There is a lagoon and Donner Lake to explore. Dogs must be leashed. The camp sites are closed for the winter. From Truckee, drive west 3 miles on Donner Pass Road. For more information, call (800) 444-PARK.

Martis Creek Wildlife Viewing Area
During the summer months, this becomes the unofficial Truckee dog park, where dogs can run leash-free. Located on Hwy 267 between Truckee and Kings Beach across from the Martis Creek Lake.

NORTH SHORE

North Tahoe Regional Park
Enjoy beautiful lakeviews while at this 300-acre state park. There are tennis courts, basketball courts and baseball fields along with miles of hiking trails. From Tahoe City, head east on Hwy 28, for 8.2 miles. Turn left on National Ave, and left on Donner Road. Follow the road to the park. $3 parking fee. For more information, call (530) 546-7248 or (530) 546-5043.

Tahoe State Recreation Area
This state recreation area has a small park with picnic tables. It is right in Tahoe City and has its own private beach which allows dogs. Located just east of the Safeway Shopping Center in Tahoe City.

Skylandia Park
This is a nice place to take your dog for a stroll. There are both a paved path and trails thru the woods. There are picnic tables overlooking Lake Tahoe. Dogs must be leashed and are not allowed on the beach. From Tahoe City, drive east on Hwy 28 for approx. 2 miles and turn right on the 2nd Lake Forest Rd. The park will be about .5 miles down on your left.

WEST SHORE

William B Layton Memorial Park
This 3-acre park in Tahoe City allows dogs to roll on its grassy lawns, and swim at its rocky beach. Enjoy your lunch at one of the picnic tables. Located right in Tahoe City behind the Bridgetender Bar & Grill.

64 Acres Park
This park is located along the Truckee River in Tahoe City. There are trails you can explore or just hang out and play in the river. From the Y in Tahoe City, drive south on Hwy 89 for .2 miles and turn right where you see the sign for 'Truckee River Access'.

INCLINE VILLAGE

Incline Village Park
Located right across from Incline Village Beach, this park often has soccer and baseball games. There are doggie dispensers with free scoopers to encourage you to clean up after your dog. From downtown Incline Village, drive east on Hwy 28 and turn right on Country Club Drive. Turn right on Lakeshore Blvd and the park is on your right.

SOUTH LAKE TAHOE

Emerald Bay State Park
Secluded from the highway, this large state park has wonderful views of the lake. Dogs must be leashed, and are only allowed in the campground and on paved roads. The camp sites are closed for the winter.. For more information, call (800) 444-PARK.

*"In the beginning God created man,
but seeing him so feeble, gave him the dog."*

–Anonymous

HIKING
TRAILS

Rascal, Golden Retriever Puppy

TRUCKEE

EASY HIKES

Donner Peak

3.5 Miles Roundtrip– Easy

Bring a picnic and enjoy the expansive views of Donner Lake and Lake Tahoe. From Truckee, drive west on the I-80 for 10.5 miles to the Soda Springs Exit. Turn left and drive past Sugar Bowl to Alpine Skills International. Turn right and drive through the parking lot to the Pacific Crest Trailhead. After parking, begin your hike at the Overland Emigrant Trail. Turn left at the Mount Judah Loop junction, and veer left at the Emigrant Wagon Trail. Continue to Emigrant Pass, turn left and hike up hill to Donner Peak.

Summit Lake

4 Miles Roundtrip– Easy

After passing through a tunnel under the freeway, you will hike through forests and fields of wildflowers. This is a great place to picnic and swim. From Truckee, drive west on I-80 approximately 8 miles and take the Castle Peak Exit. Follow the signs to the Pacific Crest Trailhead and park in the parking lot. Follow the main trail until you see a sign for Summit Lake.

MODERATE HIKES

Eagle Lakes

6 Miles Roundtrip– Moderate

This is a great spot for fishing, biking and camping. From Truckee, drive west on I-80 for 21 miles to the Eagle Lakes Exit. Go north for .5 miles and make a right on Eagle Lakes Road. Drive on this dirt road to the parking area. Park here and continue up the dirt road to the Eagle Lakes Trailhead.

Frog Point

8.5 Miles Roundtrip– Moderate
Climb through massive granite boulders and meadows of wildflowers and enjoy vistas of Donner Summit. From Truckee, drive west on I-80 for 7.5 miles to the Boreal Ridge Exit, and turn left under the freeway. Make another left and follow the signs to the Pacific Crest Trailhead. Park and begin hiking on the Pacific Crest Trail. Follow this trail until you see signs for Summit Lake/Warren Lake. Follow the signs to Warren Lake and you will begin a climb between Frog Point and Castle Peak. Turn right and continue to Frog Summit.

Loch Leven Lakes Trail

7 Miles Roundtrip– Moderate
This trail will take you over the Southern Pacific Railroad to the first of 3 small lakes. The lakes get warm enough to swim in over summer. This is a great spot for fishing and camping. From Truckee, go west on I-80 for 17 miles to the Big Bend Exit. Turn left and drive .6 miles to the parking area across from the Loch Leven Lakes Trailhead.

Pacific Crest Trail at Donner Pass

8 Miles Roundtrip– Moderate
Hike through lodgepole forests and enjoy beautiful views of Donner Lake. From Truckee, drive 10.5 miles west to the Soda Springs Exit. Turn left and drive past Sugar Bowl to Alpine Skills International. Turn right and drive through the parking lot to the Pacific Crest Trailhead. If you want to shorten this hike, you can hike one way and come out at the Pacific Crest Trail, at the Castle Peak Exit off I-80.

STRENUOUS HIKES

Mt. Lola

9 Miles Roundtrip– Strenuous
This hike will take you through willow groves, open meadows, across creeks and ponds, and you will end up at 9,148 feet elevation with breathtaking panoramic vistas. From Truckee, head north on Hwy 89 for 14.5 miles to Henness Pass Road. Drive west for 1.5 miles to Jackson Meadow. Turn left and go 0.8 miles toward Independence Lake. After crossing the river, turn right on Old Henness Pass Road. Drive 3.3 miles to the Mt. Lola Trailhead. The trail is marked along the way with white arrows in the dirt and white diamonds on the trees.

Cassidy and Fantasy, Cocker Spaniels

NORTH SHORE
EASY HIKES

Martis Peak Trail
3.5 Miles Roundtrip– Easy
Enjoy panoramic views of Lake Tahoe from this trail. From Tahoe City, drive east for 9 miles on Hwy 28 and turn left on Hwy 267. Drive north for 3.8 miles and turn left at the dirt turnout and park (.5 miles south of Brockway Summit). Cross Hwy 267 and start up the dirt road. Follow the signs for the Tahoe Rim Trail and veer left at the junction.

Squaw Creek Trail
2 Miles Roundtrip– Easy
This trail follows Squaw Creek, past a waterfall and through a meadow filled with wildflowers. From Tahoe City, drive 5 miles north on Hwy 89 and turn left on Squaw Valley Road. Drive 2.2 miles and turn right into Olympic Village. Park past the fire station. The trailhead is at the end of the Olympic Village Inn.

Truckee River Trail

9 Miles Roundtrip - Easy

This paved road follows the river from Tahoe City to the entrance of Alpine Meadows. It is a very popular path for people on bikes and roller blades, so keep your dog close. From Tahoe City, drive 0.2 miles south on Hwy 89 and park in the trailhead parking area.

MODERATE HIKES

Five Lakes Trail

5 Miles Roundtrip– Moderate

Dogs are discouraged on this popular trail. You will climb for the first 2 miles, then approach the first of 5 small lakes. There are breathtaking views of Alpine Meadows Ski Area. From Tahoe City, drive approximately 4 miles north on Hwy 89 and turn left on Alpine Meadows Road. Drive 1.5 miles and the trailhead will be on the right, across from Deer Park Drive.

Shirley Lake Trail

5 Miles Roundtrip– Moderate

Watch for stone trail markers, as you climb over large granite boulders. Stay to the left of the creek, and follow it to Shirley Lake. From Tahoe City, drive 5 miles north on Hwy 89 and turn left on Squaw Valley Road. Drive 2.5 miles and turn left toward the Squaw Valley Tram. Turn right on Squaw Peak Road and drive 0.4 miles to the trailhead.

Tahoe Rim Trail

4 Miles Roundtrip - Moderate

This hike is just a small portion of the Tahoe Rim Trail, which continues around the lake. From Tahoe City, drive north on Hwy 89, past the intersection with Hwy 28 for 0.1 miles and turn right on Fairway Drive. Follow for 0.2 miles and park in the Fairway Community Center parking lot on the right side of the road. The trailhead is located just across the street. Follow the trail markers. For more information, call the Tahoe Rim Trail Association at (775) 588-0686.

WEST SHORE
EASY HIKES

Eagle Rock

1.5 Miles Roundtrip– Easy

Bring your camera! There are spectacular views from up here. This is a great hike for late afternoon. From Tahoe City, drive south 4.2 miles on Hwy 89 and turn right on Blackwood Canyon Road. The trail begins a quarter mile in on the left. Follow the power lines that climb up a ridge to the south, then veer to the east up Eagle Rock.

Granite Lake Trail

2 Miles Roundtrip – Easy

You will enjoy beautiful vistas of Lake Tahoe while hiking up this steep trail. The lake is a great spot for swimming and fishing. A wilderness permit is required for this hike. From Tahoe City, drive south on Hwy 89 for 19 miles to the Bayview Trailhead and Campground. Park and follow the Bayview Trail and veer right at the Cascade Falls Trail. At the next junction go left to Granite Lake.

Page Meadows

14 Miles of Trails – Easy

There are about 14 miles of trails in this area that will take you to scenic Page Meadows. From Tahoe City, drive south on Hwy 89 for .5 miles and turn right on Granlibakken Road. Turn left on Rawhide Drive and park at the end of the road. Go through the gates and along the fire road.

Maggie, Black Lab Mix

MODERATE HIKES

Ellis Peak Trail

5 Miles Roundtrip– Moderate

You will hike through forest and meadows, and along the way, see beautiful views of the lake. When the trail splits, go left to Ellis Lake, or right to Ellis Peak. From Tahoe City, drive south on Hwy 89 for 4.2 miles. Turn right on Blackwood Canyon Road, and drive approximately 7 miles until you reach Barker Pass. The trail starts on the south side of the road where the pavement ends.

STRENUOUS HIKES

Crag Lake
10 Miles Roundtrip– Strenuous
This trail takes you into beautiful Desolation Wilderness. Enjoy a variety of wildflowers in the spring. Bring a lunch and eat atop one of the many granite boulders that overlook the lake. A wilderness permit is required for this hike. From Tahoe City, drive south on Hwy 89 for 11 miles to Meeks Bay and park near the Desolation Wilderness Trailhead. Begin your hike down the gated dirt road and veer right at the Tahoe-Yosemite Trail sign. You will pass a small lake, then continue another couple of miles to Crag Lake.

Tahoe Rim Trail - Barker Pass to Tahoe City
13 Miles One Way - Strenuous
You will pass the Granite Chief Wilderness, Blackwood Canyon and Ward Canyon. You will enjoy the spectacular vistas of Lake Tahoe as you hike by a waterfall, thru big open meadows and across many streams. From Tahoe City, drive about 5 miles south on Hwy 89 and turn right on Blackwood Canyon Road. Follow 7 miles to the top of Blackwood Canyon and park at the Pacific Crest Trailhead. Begin at the trailhead on the right side and follow the Tahoe Rim Trail markers. Don't forget to leave a car on the other end. Leave one car at the 64 Acres parking lot, approximately 0.2 miles south of the Tahoe City Y, on Hwy 89 on the right. For more information, call the Tahoe Rim Trail Association at (775) 588-0686.

Velma Lakes Trail
11 Miles Roundtrip– Strenuous
You will pass beautiful Eagle Lake on your way to Upper, Middle and Lower Velma Lakes. This is a great spot for swimming and camping. A wilderness permit is required for this hike in Desolation Wilderness. From Tahoe City, drive south on Hwy 89 for 18 miles to Emerald Bay. Make a right at the Eagle Falls Trailhead parking lot. Start on the Eagle Falls Trail and veer left at the Velma Lakes Trail sign.

Ward Creek Canyon
12 Miles Roundtrip– Strenuous
This trail will take you to the top of Twin Peaks with views of Lake Tahoe and the Granite Chief Wilderness. From Tahoe City, drive south on Hwy 89 for 3.2 miles and turn right on Pineland Drive. Turn left on Twin Peaks Road, then follow the signs to Ward Creek Canyon. Drive to the Forest Service Road 15N62 and park. Walk left down the forest service road and follow the signs for Twin Peaks Trail.

INCLINE VILLAGE

EASY HIKES

Skunk Harbor
3 Miles Roundtrip– Easy
This hike will take you down to the beautiful shoreline of east Lake Tahoe. There is plenty to explore, including The Newhall House, a historic stone house that was built in the 1920's and is now owned by the U.S. Forest Service. This private cove makes a great place for picnicking and swimming. From Tahoe City, drive east on Hwy 28 for 24 miles. Park on the right side of the road, just past Skunk Harbor, at the gated fire road. Follow the trail down the fire road.

MODERATE HIKES

Mount Rose Trail
12 Miles Roundtrip– Moderate
You will hike through fields of wildflowers and along winding creeks. Enjoy spectacular views of Carson City, Lake Tahoe and even Donner Lake. From Incline Village, drive north on Hwy 431 (Mt. Rose Highway) for 7.6 miles to a gated dirt road on the left side of the highway. Park and start your hike up the dirt road. Turn right at the Big Meadow Trail junction to get to the top of Mount Rose.

STRENUOUS HIKES

Tahoe Rim Trail - Mt. Rose to Spooner Lake
21 Miles One Way - Strenuous

This section of the Tahoe Rim Trail takes you along the ridgeline above the east shore of Lake Tahoe. There are spectacular views of the lake along the way. This trail is very dry, so bring lots of water. The hike is long, but the terrain is not difficult. This spot is popular for mountain bikers. From Incline Village, drive north on Hwy 431 (Mt. Rose Highway) for 6.5 miles to the trailhead, just below Tahoe Meadows. Park on the side of the road and follow the signs for the Tahoe Rim Trail. Don't forget to leave a car at the other end. You will come out at the Spooner North Trailhead on the north side of Hwy 50, about .5 miles east of the Hwy 28 intersection. For more information, call the Tahoe Rim Trail Association at (775) 588-0686.

Maurice, Golden Retriever

SOUTH LAKE TAHOE

EASY HIKES

Angora Lakes Trail

1 Mile Roundtrip – Easy

This short hike is a great spot for lunch and a swim. You will reach Lower Angora Lake after 0.25 miles and Upper Angora Lake after 0.5 miles. Angora Lakes Resort has boats for rent and a snack bar. From the Y in South Lake Tahoe, drive north on Hwy 89 for 3 miles and turn left on to Fallen Leaf Lake Road. Drive for 2 miles and turn left on Tahoe Mountain Road. Follow for approximately 0.4 miles and turn right at Forest Service Road #1214. Drive for 3 miles to the trailhead and park. Begin your hike at the trailhead at the south end of the parking lot.

Cascade Falls Trail

2 Miles Roundtrip – Easy

This trail will take you to Cascade Falls overlooking Cascade Lake. Be careful, the rocks can be slippery. Follow the creek upstream and enjoy the large granite boulders and water hole. A wilderness permit is required for this hike. From the South Lake Tahoe Y, drive north on Hwy 89 for 9.5 miles and turn left into the Bayview Trailhead and Campground. From Tahoe City, drive south on Hwy 89 for 19 miles to the Bayview Trailhead and Campground. Park and follow the Bay View Trail and veer right at the Cascade Falls Trail.

Eagle Falls Trail

3 Miles Roundtrip– Easy

You will follow a creek and pass a breathtaking waterfall, as you approach Eagle Lake which is surrounded by gigantic granite cliffs. A wilderness permit is required for this hike. From Tahoe City, drive south on Hwy 89 for 18 miles to Emerald Bay. Turn right at the Eagle Falls parking area. Begin your hike at the Eagle Falls Trailhead.

Fallen Leaf Lake Trail
3.5 Miles Roundtrip –Easy
This beautiful lake is a great spot for picnicking, swimming, fishing, and biking. From the South Lake Tahoe Y, drive north on Hwy 89 and turn left on Fallen Leaf Lake Road. Follow the road past the campground to the Fallen Leaf Lake Trailhead.

Horsetail Falls
2.4 Miles Roundtrip - Easy
This waterfall is a spectacular sight! The trail can be difficult to follow because it crosses many large granite slabs. From the South Lake Tahoe Y, drive southwest on Hwy 50 for 16 miles, past Echo Summit to Twin Bridges. Park in the parking lot on the right and begin your hike at the Twin Bridges Trailhead.

Lam Watah Interpretive Trail
2 Miles Roundtrip – Easy
This 1 mile trail takes you through a large open field and has interpretive signs which give you historic facts on the Washoe Indians who used to live in this area and information on local vegetation. The path takes you to Nevada Beach. From the casinos, drive east on Hwy 50 for 0.8 miles. Turn left on Kahle Dr. and the parking lot will be immediately on you right.

Tallac Historic Site
2 Miles Roundtrip – Easy
Follow the path along the lake where you can tour the Washoe Gardens, Baldwin Estate, Pope Estate, Valhalla Estate, and the Taylor Creek Visitors Center. Dogs are not allowed inside any of the estates. There are picnic tables, if you would like to bring a lunch. Dogs are allowed to swim in the lake around Kiva picnic area, but there is only about 2 feet of beach. They are not allowed in the Taylor Creek Marsh. Dogs must be on leash. From the South Lake Tahoe Y, drive north on Hwy 89 for 3 miles and turn right at the Tallac Historic Site/Kiva Beach sign. Park in the lot and begin your hike on the Historic Estates Trail at the end of the parking lot. For more information, call (530) 573-2600.

The Hawley Grade Trail

3.5 Miles Roundtrip – Easy

This historic hike is on the first wagon road built in the area in the late 1850's. The trails follows the Upper Truckee River. From South Lake Tahoe Y, drive south on Hwy 50 for 5.3 miles and turn left on South Upper Truckee Road. Drive 3.5 miles and turn at the Hawley Grade sign. Continue to the end of the road and park past the houses.

MODERATE HIKES

Big Meadows Trail

6 Miles Roundtrip– Moderate

This trail takes you through a large, open meadow that's filled with beautiful wildflowers in spring. A creek follows the trail, which your dog will enjoy cooling off in on a hot summer day. The trail comes out at Round Lake, which is lined with large granite boulders. Bring a leash, you will need to cross the highway. From South Lake Tahoe Y, drive south on Hwy 50 for 4.5 miles to the stop light. Turn left on Hwy 89 and drive south for 5.5 miles to the Big Meadows Trailhead. Park and follow the trail at the south side of the lot. Safely cross the highway and find the trail on the other side of the road.

Cathedral Lake

4.5 Miles Roundtrip – Moderate

You will follow the Mount Tallac Trail past Floating Island Lake to Cathedral Lake. There are beautiful views of Fallen Leaf Lake and Lake Tahoe. Stay on the main trail and follow the signs to Cathedral lake. A Wilderness Permit is required for this hike into Desolation Wilderness. From the South Lake Tahoe Y, drive north on Hwy 89 for 4 miles and turn left at the Mount Tallac Trailhead. Follow the signs to the parking lot and begin your hike at the trailhead.

Emigrant Lake Trail

8 Miles Roundtrip – Moderate

The trail follows the shoreline of Caples Lake then climbs along Emigrant Creek. After passing through an open meadow and dense forest, you will arrive at Emigrant Lake which is surrounded by large granite boulders. Beautiful views of Kirkwood Ski Resort. From South Lake Tahoe Y, drive 4.5 miles south on Hwy 50 to the stop light. Turn left and follow Hwy 89 south for 11 miles to Hwy 88. Follow Hwy 88 towards Carson Pass 13.5 miles to the parking area, just past Caples Lake. Park and begin hiking at the Emigrant Lake Trailhead at the south end of the parking lot.

Fountain Place Trail

4 Miles Roundtrip – Moderate

This trail passes through Fountain Place, an open meadow with beautiful wildflowers in spring. The climb is short and steep, with over 1700 feet of elevation gain. Enjoy the views from the top. From South Lake Tahoe Y, drive south on Hwy 50 for 4 miles and turn left on Pioneer Road. Turn right on Oneidas Street and drive to the end, where it becomes a Forest Service Road. Continue on this road until the pavement ends, approximately 4 miles. Park and follow the dirt road.

Glen Alpine Trail

5 Miles Roundtrip – Moderate

This trail takes you through forests and past lakes, creeks and waterfalls. You will end up at Grass Lake in Desolation Wilderness. The trail is clearly marked with signs. A wilderness permit is required for this hike. From South Lake Tahoe Y, drive north on Hwy 89 for 3 miles and turn left on to Fallen Leaf Lake Road. Drive for 5 miles past the Fallen Leaf Lake Marnia and veer left at the fork in the road on to Forest Service Road #1216. Follow the signs for Lilly Lake, over a bridge and park at the trailhead. Start your hike at the green metal Forest Service gate.

Subaru & Satchel, Malamute/Wolf mix

Lake Margaret Trail

5 Miles Roundtrip– Moderate

This trail takes you through forests of Pine and meadows of wildflowers. This is a great spot for a picnic and a swim. The trail is marked with white diamonds and arrows. From South Lake Tahoe Y, drive 4.5 miles south on Hwy 50 to the stop light. Turn left on Hwy 89 and drive south for 11 miles to Hwy 88. Drive towards Carson Pass for 13.6 miles and turn right at a paved road between Caples Lake and Kirkwood Ski Resort. Park near the Lake Margaret Trailhead.

Ralston Peak Trail

8 Miles Roundtrip – Moderate

This scenic hike into Desolation Wilderness gives you beautiful views of Horsetail Falls, one of the most breathtaking waterfalls in Lake Tahoe. A wilderness permit is required for this hike. From South Lake Tahoe Y, drive 13.5 miles south on Hwy 50 and turn right at Camp Sacramento. Drive down this dirt road and park at the church. The Ralston Peak Trailhead is on the left side of the road.

Susie Lake Trail

8 Miles Roundtrip – Moderate

This scenic trail in Desolation Wilderness passes by creeks and waterfalls. Continue another mile past Susie Lake to reach Heather Lake, and another 2 miles to reach Lake Aloha. A wilderness permit is required for this hike. From South Lake Tahoe Y, drive north 3 miles on Hwy 89 and turn left on Fallen Leaf Lake Road. Pass the Fallen Leaf Lodge and continue down the Forest Service Road. Follow the signs toward Lily Lake to the Glen Alpine Trailhead. Park and begin hiking on the gravel road, following the signs to Susie Lake.

STRENUOUS HIKES

Aloha Lake Loop

12 Miles Roundtrip - Strenuous

The first few miles of this hike are extremely steep. You will pass by almost a dozen lakes with lots of opportunities for a quick dip. From South Lake Tahoe Y, drive north on Hwy 89 and turn left on Fallen Leaf Lake Road. Follow this road for approximately 5.2 miles to the wilderness area at the end of the road and park in the trailhead parking lot. Start your hike at the trailhead about 1/4 mile back on Fallen Leaf Lake Road. Follow the signs to Aloha Lake.

Echo Lakes Trail

12 Miles Roundtrip – Strenuous

You will begin at Lower Echo Lake and end at Lake Aloha. This is one of the most spectacular hikes in the area! Bring your camera and enjoy the scenery. Over summer, you and your dog can take the water taxi that crosses Echo Lake, and shorten your hike by 5 miles. A wilderness permit is required for this hike. From South Lake Tahoe Y, drive south on Hwy 50 for 9.6 miles and turn right on Echo Lakes Road. Continue to an intersection and turn left. Park in the upper lot at the Echo Lakes Resort. The water taxi leaves from the boat dock at the Echo Lakes Resort. For information on the water taxi, call (530) 659-7207.

Freel Meadows Trail

12 Miles Roundtrip – Strenuous

This scenic trail takes you along creeks, through dense forests and beside large granite slabs. You will end up at Hellhole Vista, where you can enjoy beautiful views of the Carson Range. From South Lake Tahoe Y, drive south on Hwy 50 for 4.5 miles to the stop light. Turn left on Hwy 89 and drive south for 5.5 miles to the Big Meadows Trailhead. Park in the main trailhead parking area. From the Big Meadow Trailhead, follow the blue diamonds that mark the Tahoe Rim Trail. Continue and follow the signs to Freel Meadows and Hellhole Vista.

Mount Tallac

10 Miles Roundtrip – Strenuous

You will climb 5 miles and gain over 3,000 feet of elevation to arrive at the top of Mount Tallac, where you will have truly unbelievable views of all of Lake Tahoe. You will pass 2 lakes, which are a great spot for a picnic lunch. Bring a jacket, it can get cold at the top. A wilderness permit is required for this hike. From South Lake Tahoe Y, drive north on Hwy 89 for 3.5 miles. Turn left on the dirt road at the Mount Tallac Trailhead sign across from Baldwin Beach.

*No one appreciates the very special genius
of your conversation as the dog does.*

–Christopher Morley

MOUNTAIN
BIKING

Krystal Bear, Pit Bull

TRUCKEE

Carr, Feely and Lindsey Lakes Trails

There are miles and miles of hiking and mountain biking trails in this area, all that allow dogs. You will pass by many small lakes, including Lindsey Lake, Feely Lake, Milk Lake, Hidden Lake and Island Lake, where you can swim out to one of many islands. Be cautious of hikers. The following are some of the trails in this area:

Rock Lake– 8.5 Miles Roundtrip. Turn towards "Lindsey Lakes" on the road into the campground. Park at the campground and follow the fire road.

Penner Lake– 6.5 Miles Roundtrip. Turn towards "Carr and Feely Lake" on the road into the campground. Park in the lot and begin down the fire road on the south side of the campground. Follow the signs for Round Lake Trail to Crooked Lakes Trail. Continue on this trail to Penner Lake.

Shotgun Lake– 8 Miles Roundtrip. Turn towards "Carr and Feely Lake" on the road to the campground. Park in the lot and begin down the fire road at the south end of the campground. Follow Round Lake Trail and turn left on Grouse Ridge Trail, which will take you to Shotgun Lake.

DIRECTIONS: From Truckee, drive west on I-80 for 23 miles to the Nevada City Exit and go south. Drive for 4 miles on Route 20 and turn right on Bowman Road. Drive 8.5 miles to Forest Service Road #17. Turn right and follow the signs to Carr and Feely Lakes or go left to "Lindsey Lakes". (Note: 4WD needed on this road).

Eagle Lakes/ Indian Springs Trails

There are many miles of hiking and mountain biking trails here that allow dogs. Be cautious of hikers. The following are 2 trails in this area:

Eagle Lakes– 6 Miles Roundtrip. This trail takes you to Eagle Lakes which is a great spot for camping.

Footfalls– 12 Miles Roundtrip. This trail leads to a beautiful waterfall and swimming hole. Use caution near the waterfall, the rocks can be slippery.

DIRECTIONS: From Truckee, drive west on I-80 for 20.5 miles to the Eagles Lake Exit. Go north for 0.5 miles and make a right on Eagle Lakes Road. Drive 0.2 miles on this dirt road to the parking area. Park here and continue up the dirt road to the Eagle Lakes Trailhead.

Mt. Lola

This strenuous 13 mile trail will take you through willow groves, open meadows, across creeks and ponds, and you will end up at 9,148 feet elevation with breathtaking panoramic vistas. From Truckee, head north on Hwy 89 for 14.5 miles to Henness Pass Road. Drive west for 1.5 miles to Jackson Meadow. Turn left at the sign for Independence Lake. After crossing the bridge, turn right on Old Henness Pass Road. Drive 3.3 miles to the Mt. Lola Trailhead. The trail is marked along the way with white arrows in the dirt and white diamonds on the trees.

NORTH SHORE

Martis Peak Trail

For an intermediate ride, bike 6 miles roundtrip to Martis Peak Lookout. For a more advanced ride, bike 12 miles roundtrip to the top of Mt. Baldy. Enjoy panoramic lakeviews of all of Lake Tahoe from this trail. From Tahoe City, drive east on Hwy 28 for 9 miles and turn left on Hwy 267. Drive just past Brockway Summit, and look for a dirt road on your right. Park at the entrance and follow the dirt road.

Mount Watson Peak Trail

There are about 11 miles of trails and fire roads throughout this area. Check out the views at the top of Mount Watson! From Tahoe City, drive east on Hwy 28 for 2.5 miles and turn left on Fabian Way (just before the Shell Gas Station). Turn right on Village Road and left on Country Club Drive. Drive to the Lakeview Nordic Ski Area and park by the building. From the parking lot, go past the gate and down the fire road.

Squaw Valley

Grab your bike and your dog and head for Squaw Valley. You can take the tram to the top and mountain bike with your dog on one of the numerous trails. From Tahoe City, drive 5 miles north on Hwy 89 and turn left on Squaw Valley Road. Park in the lot and head towards the tram. Dogs must be leashed on the tram. $16 for adults, dogs are free. For more information, call (530) 583-6985.

Truckee River Bike Path

This paved path goes from Tahoe City to Squaw Valley and is about 5 miles long. Your dog will enjoy taking a dip in the Truckee River after the 5-mile ride. Dogs must be leashed. The path starts at the intersection between Hwy 89 and Hwy 28 in Tahoe City.

Western States Trail

There are about 10 miles of trails in this area for you and your dog to explore. Hop on that bike and enjoy the challenging uphill and the exhilarating downhill of this ride, which has beautiful views of the lake. From Tahoe City, drive north on Hwy 89 for 4.5 miles to the parking area by the Alpine Meadows Bridge on the left side of the road. Park and start down the paved bike path under the bridge, heading north and follow the signs to the Western States Trail.

WEST SHORE

Barker Pass

There are almost 30 miles of trails in this area, off of Blackwood Canyon Road. Follow the trails to Ellis Lake and Ellis Peak. Be cautious of hikers. From Tahoe City, drive south on Hwy 89 for 4 miles to Blackwood Canyon Road (Kaspian Campground). Continue on Blackwood Canyon Road for 2.5 miles, until the road splits. Instead of following the paved road over the bridge, continue straight on the dirt road. There will be parking on the right. Begin down the fire road through the gate.

Blackwood Canyon Road

There are about 15 miles of paved roads for your biking pleasure. The road is level for the first 2.5 miles and then gets steep. Be cautious of cars, this area can get busy over summer. From Tahoe City, drive south on Hwy 89 for 4 miles to Blackwood Canyon Road (Kaspian Campground). There is a parking area on the right.

General Creek

This 6 mile trail is nice and level, perfect for the kids and the dog. From Tahoe City, drive 9.2 miles south on Hwy 89 to the General Creek Campground. There is a $3 fee at the entrance gate. Park in the visitor's parking lot. Begin down the paved bike path and veer right at the dirt trail. Maps available at the entrance gate.

Page Meadows

There are about 14 miles of trails in this area that will take you to scenic Page Meadows. Be cautious of hikers. From Tahoe City, drive south on Hwy 89 for 0.5 miles and turn right on Granlibakken Road. Turn left on Rawhide Drive and park at the end of the road. Go through the gates and along the fire road.

Ward Creek Canyon

This moderate 12 mile trail will take you to the top of Twin Peaks with views of Lake Tahoe, Ward Creek Canyon, and the Granite Chief Wilderness. From Tahoe City, drive south on Hwy 89 for 3.2 miles and turn right on Pineland Drive. Turn left on Twin Peaks Road, then follow the signs to Ward Creek Canyon. Drive to the Forest Service Road 15N62 and park. Start your ride left down the forest service road and follow the signs for Twin Peaks Trail.

INCLINE VILLAGE

Marlette Lake – Flume Trail

There are 16 miles of trails in this area for mountain biking with your dog. You'll start at Spooner Lake, and continue up past Marlette Lake to the Flume Trail. The trail comes out by the Ponderosa Ranch, so either leave one car there, or return to where you started. From Incline Village, drive south on Hwy 28 for approximately 12 miles to Spooner Lake- Nevada State Park. There is a $5 fee at the entrance gate. Park and follow the signs for Marlette Lake/ Flume Trail.

Ophir Creek Trail

This is a great spot for children. The trail is 3 miles each way, and is almost completely level. This trail takes you through Tahoe Meadows, where you can enjoy the wildflowers, and your dog can enjoy the creek that follows along the trail. From Incline Village, drive north on Hwy 431 (Mount Rose Hwy) for 6.5 miles. You will see a large open meadow on your right. Park on the side of the road and find the trail by the creek.

Tandra, Malamute/Sheppard mix
Beauregard, Great Dane/Sheppard mix

SOUTH LAKE TAHOE

Angora Lakes Trail

This easy, 8 mile roundtrip bike ride follows a fire road to Angora Lakes. Be cautious of off-road vehicles. Boat rentals are available at the lake. From the South Lake Tahoe Y, drive north on Hwy 89 for 3 miles. Turn left on Fallen Leaf Lake Road and left on Tahoe Mountain Road. Park near Angora Ridge Road, which is a dirt road.

Lake Margaret Trail

This trail is easy and fun. Five miles roundtrip with many hills and dips along the way. Be cautious of hikers. The trail is marked with white diamonds and arrows. From South Lake Tahoe Y, drive south for 4.5 miles on Hwy 50 to the stop light. Turn left on Hwy 89 and drive south for 11 miles to Hwy 88. Drive towards Carson Pass for 13.6 miles and turn right at a paved road between Caples Lake and Kirkwood Ski Resort. Park near the Lake Margaret Trailhead.

Mr. Toad's Wild Ride

This 16 mile roundtrip ride is steep at times and can be difficult. Be cautious of slippery rocks. From the South Lake Tahoe Y, drive south on Hwy 50 for 4 miles and turn left on Pioneer Road. Turn right on Oneidas Street, drive through the gate and continue until the road becomes a paved forest service road. Park near the Saxon Creek Bridge. Begin your ride up the paved road, following the trail through the gate and continue on the dirt road.

Money will buy you a pretty good dog,
but it won't buy you the wag of his tail.

–Henry Wheeler Shaw

CROSS COUNTRY SKIING

Oscar, German Sheppard mix

TRUCKEE

Big Bend
There are unmarked trails running all over this area near the Yuba River. Be cautious of snowmobiles. From Truckee drive west on I-80 for 17 miles to the Big Bend Exit. Turn left on Hampshire Rocks Road and park in the parking lot. Begin at the trailhead.

Cabin Creek Trail
This trail has some steep areas and is for more advanced cross country skiers. Be cautious of snowmobiles. 9 Mile Loop. From Truckee, drive south on Hwy 89 for 3 miles to Cabin Creek Road. Turn right and drive 1 mile to the trailhead. Park on the side of the road.

Donner Memorial State Park
Dogs are not allowed on the main groomed cross country trail, but they are allowed on smaller side trails. A sno-park permit is needed to park here. Parking and permit available at the on-site museum. From Truckee, take the Donner Lake Exit off of I-80 and follow signs to the park.

Sagehen Trail
This unmarked trail is for more advanced cross country skiers and their dogs. Be cautious of snowmobiles. 5 Mile Loop. From Truckee, drive north on Hwy 89 for 8 miles to Sagehen Summit. Park in the lot on the west side of the road.

Royal Gorge
Dogs are allowed on the 2 Van Norden groomed trails on Saturdays and Sundays. Dogs may be off-leash if they are under strict voice control, but they prefer if your dog wears a harness. A doggie day pass is $5. Royal Gorge is located in Soda Springs, just outside of Truckee. For more information, call (800) 666-3871 or (530) 426-3871.

NORTH SHORE

Martis Peak Trail
This intermediate trail is unmarked and continues for 3.5 miles (one way). Enjoy panoramic lakeviews of all of Lake Tahoe from this trail. From Tahoe City, drive east for 9 miles on Hwy 28 and turn left on Hwy 267. Drive north for 3.8 miles and turn left at the dirt turnout and park (0.5 miles south of Brockway Summit). Cross Hwy 267 and start up the dirt road. Follow the signs for the Tahoe Rim Trail and veer left at the junction.

North Tahoe Regional Park
Enjoy beautiful lakeviews while cross country skiing with your dog on one of the many trails in this 300-acre park. Be cautious of snowmobiles. From Tahoe City, head east on Hwy 28, for 8.2 miles. Turn left on National Ave, and left on Donner Road. Follow the road to the park. $3 parking fee. For more information, call (530) 546-7248 or (530) 546-5043.

Tahoe Cross Country Season Pass for Dogs
Now you can cross country ski with your pooch on groomed trails! There are 2 trails open to dogs, which are allowed leash-free but under voice control. Doggie bags are provided for cleaning up messes. Dogs are allowed Mon - Fri 8:30am - 5:00pm and Saturday, Sunday and Holidays 2:00pm - 5:00pm. A season pass is $45 for 1 dog and $75 for 2 dogs. Day passes are also available at $3 per day per dog. For more information, call (530) 583.5475. Located at 925 Country Club Dr., Tahoe City.

WEST SHORE

Blackwood Canyon Road
This road is gated off over winter. The first 2.5 miles are flat, a great spot for beginners. If you would like more of a challenge, the trail continues another 7 miles and gets steeper and more difficult. Be cautious of snowmobiles. From Tahoe City, drive south on Hwy 89 for 3 miles to Blackwood Canyon Road, near the Kaspian Recreation Area. You will find the parking area on the right. A sno-park permit is needed to park here.

McKinney Rubicon Springs

This trail is unmarked and will take you through the forest and past several small lakes. Be cautious of snowmobiles. 6 Miles Roundtrip. From Tahoe City, drive south on Hwy 89 for approximately 9 miles and turn right on McKinney Rubicon Springs Road. Veer left to Bellvue Drive and turn right on McKinney Road. Turn left on McKinney Rubicon Springs Road. The trail begins at the end of the road.

Page Meadows

This unmarked trail for intermediates will take you and your dog to a big open meadow. From Tahoe City, drive south on Hwy 89 for about 3 miles. Turn right on Pine St. and veer right on Tahoe Park Heights Drive. Continue up the steep hill (you may need 4WD or chains) and turn right on Big Pine Drive. Make your first left on Silver Tip Drive. Go to the end of the paved road and park. The trail starts at the end of Silver Tip Drive.

INCLINE VILLAGE

Tahoe Meadows

This large, flat meadow is a great spot for you and your dog to cross country ski. There are about 6 miles of trails. Be cautious of snowmobiles. From Incline Village, head west on Hwy 28 to Hwy 431 (Mount Rose Highway). Turn right and drive for 6.5 miles to the large flat meadow on the right side of the road and park.

SOUTH LAKE TAHOE

Angora Road

This trail is 8 miles roundtrip and is for the intermediate cross country skier. You will ski through woods and past several small lakes. Be cautious of snowmobilers. From South Lake Tahoe Y, drive south for 2.5 miles on Hwy 50 and turn right on Tahoe Mountain Road. Turn right on Glenmore Way and left on Dundee Circle. Follow to the end of the road, where the trail begins down a fire road on your left.

Echo Lakes

This trail is for intermediate cross country skiers and their dogs. There are many trails in this area, most which lead to Upper and Lower Echo Lakes. A map of the trails can be picked up at the Forest Service Office. A sno-park permit is needed to park here. From South Lake Tahoe Y, drive south on Hwy 50 for 9.6 miles and turn right on Echo Lakes Road. Park in the Echo Lakes Sno-Park area.

Fountain Place

There are six miles of trails (one way) for the more advanced cross country skier. Be cautious of snowmobilers. From South Lake Tahoe Y, drive south on Hwy 50 for 4 miles and turn left on Pioneer Road. Turn right on Oneidas Street and drive to the end, where it becomes a Forest Service Road. Continue on this road until the pavement ends, approximately 4 miles. The trail starts at the end of the road.

Grass Lake Meadow

This is a great spot for beginners. There are about 3 miles of flat, open meadow for you and your dog. From South Lake Tahoe Y, drive south for 4.5 miles on Hwy 50 to the stop light. Turn left on Hwy 89 and drive to Luther Pass and park on the side of the road.

Taylor Creek Sno-Park

There are trails for all levels of cross country skiers in this sno-park. No snowmobiles allowed on these trails. From the South Lake Tahoe Y, drive north on Hwy 89 for 3.5 miles to the sno-park. A sno-park permit is needed to park here.

In the beginning God created man,
but seeing him so feeble, gave him the dog.

–Anonymous

SLEDDING HILLS

Sierra, Vizsla

TRUCKEE

Glenshire
This is an unofficial snow play area. From downtown Truckee, drive east on Donner Pass Road and turn right on Glenshire Drive. The sledding hill is down 5 miles on the west side of the road.

Truckee
This is an unofficial snow sledding spot that is used by locals. From downtown Truckee drive 1/4 mile west on Donner Pass Road.

NORTH SHORE

Brockway Summit
This is an unofficial snow sledding spot that is used by locals. From Tahoe City, drive east on Hwy 28 for 9 miles and turn left on Hwy 267. The sledding hill is located 0.8 miles south of Northstar on Hwy 267.

North Tahoe Regional Park
There are both beginner and intermediate sledding hills at this snow park. From Tahoe City, head east on Hwy 28 for 8.2 miles. Turn left on National Ave, and left on Donner Road. Follow the road to the park. Parking- $3. Sledding- $5 per person with sled rental, $3 per person without sled rental. For more information, call (530) 546-7248 or (530) 546-6115.

Tahoe City
This is an unofficial snow sledding spot that is used by locals. From Tahoe City Y, drive south on Hwy 89 for 0.2 mile. The sledding hill is on the lake side of the highway.

INCLINE VILLAGE

Tahoe Meadows

This is an unofficial snow sledding spot that is often used by locals. From Incline Village, head west on Hwy 28 to Hwy 431 (Mount Rose Highway). Turn right and drive for 6.5 miles to the parking area on the right side of the road.

Spooner Summit

This unofficial snow sledding spot is steep, so don't bring your small children. From Incline Village drive south on Hwy 28 for about 9 miles to the junction with Hwy 50. The sledding hill is on the west side of the highway.

Incline Village

This unofficial snow sledding spot is great for beginners, and is located on the Incline Village Golf Course. The hill is on the driving range, next to The Chateau. From Incline Village, drive east on Hwy 28 and turn left on Country Club Drive.

SOUTH LAKE TAHOE

Echo Summit Sno-Park

This sno-park has a large area for snow sledding. From South Lake Tahoe Y, drive south on Hwy 50 about 10 miles to Meyers. Look for the Echo Summit Sno-Park sign and park in the lot. A sno-park permit is needed to park here.

Taylor Creek Sno-Park

This sno-park has a small sledding hill. From South Lake Tahoe Y, drive north on Hwy 89 for 3 miles. The sno-park will be on your left near Camp Richardson. A sno-park permit needed to park here.

*A dog teaches a boy fidelity, perseverance
and to turn around three times before lying down.*

–Robert Benchley

SWIMMING
SPOTS

Samantha, Black Lab mix

TRUCKEE

Martis Creek Lake
This lake is a great spot to picnic while your dog takes a swim. From Truckee, drive south on Hwy 267 for approximately 5 miles. Turn left at the Martis Creek Lake sign, and drive 0.5 miles to the lake.

Truckee River in Glenshire
A nice place to cool your dog on a hot summer day. From Truckee, drive east on Donner Pass Road past downtown and turn right on Glenshire Drive. Go 4.5 miles and turn right just past Glenshire Bridge. Follow the dirt road and park near the river.

NORTH SHORE

Coon St. Beach
This beach is small, but large enough to make any water dog happy. Bring your lunch and eat at one of the picnic tables. From Tahoe City, drive east on Hwy 28 for 9.2 miles to Kings Beach and turn left on Coon St.

Lake Forest Beach & Campground
This rocky dog beach is not pretty, but hey, it's water. There is a boat ramp next to the beach. From Tahoe City, drive east on Hwy 28 for approximately 2 miles and turn right on Lake Forest Road. Turn at the Coast Guard sign and veer right to the campground area. The beach is on your left.

Tahoe State Recreation Area
This is a campground in Tahoe City that has its own private beach which allows dogs. Located just east of the Safeway Shopping Center in Tahoe City, on Hwy 28.

Watson Lake

A great place for you to have a picnic, and for your dog to take a swim.
You'll need 4-wheel drive to get to this lake. From Tahoe City, drive east on
Hwy 28 for 9 miles and turn left on Hwy 267. Drive to the top of Brockway
Summit and turn left at the summit on the dirt road. Follow the dirt road
for 6.5 miles and turn left at another dirt road, marked 16N50 or 6/30. This
will take you to Watson Lake.

William B Layton Memorial Park

This 3 acre park in Tahoe City allows dogs to roll on its grassy lawns,
and swim at its rocky beach. Enjoy some lunch at one of the picnic tables.
Located right in Tahoe City behind the Bridgetender Bar & Grill.

Alpine Meadows Rescue Dogs - Golden Retrievers

WEST SHORE

64 Acres Park
This park is located along the Truckee River in Tahoe City. There are trails you can explore or just hang out and play in the river. From the Tahoe City Y, drive south on Hwy 89 for 0.2 miles and turn right where you see the sign for 'Truckee River Access'.

Blackwood Canyon
The landscape here is breathtaking! You and your dog can hike upstream, or stay and play in the water hole. The creek tends to be dry in late summer. From Tahoe City, drive south on Hwy 89 for 4.2 miles and turn right on Blackwood Canyon Road. Veer to the left and park near the bridge.

Hurricane Beach
This 'designated dog beach' is about 50 feet of beach right on the highway. If your dog tends to wander stay away from this beach. From Tahoe City, drive south on Hwy 89 for approximately 4 miles.

Lake Tahoe Basin Beach
This beach is small, but is a great spot for a quick dip. Bring a lunch and eat on the picnic table. The beach is located between Tahoe Shores Condos and Tahoe Tavern Condos. From the Y in Tahoe City, drive south on Hwy 89 for 0.1 mile and turn left at the 'National Forest - Lake Tahoe Basin Beach' sign. There is a very small parking lot. Follow the trail to the lake.

William Kent Beach
Located just across the street from the William Kent Campground and just north of Sunnyside Resort. There are picnic tables and lots of pine trees. From the Tahoe City Y, drive south on Hwy 89 for approximately 2 miles and turn left into the small parking lot, just before Sunnyside Resort.

INCLINE VILLAGE

Incline Village Beach
The beautiful Incline Village Beach is open to dogs in the off season, November 15th through April 15th. There are doggie dispensers with free scoopers to encourage you to clean up after your dog. From downtown Incline Village, drive east on Hwy 28 and turn right on Country Club Drive. Turn right on Lakeshore Blvd and turn left into the second gated beach.

East Shore Beaches
The East Shore has some of the most spectacular beaches on the lake. You and your dog can swim out to one of the many rocks that stick out from the crystal clear water. From Incline Village, drive east on Hwy 28, past the residential area. The beaches are scattered along the highway and are hard to see. When you see cars parked on the side of the road, park and walk towards the lake. There will be a trail that leads to the beach.

SOUTH LAKE TAHOE

Cove East
This is a great spot to go for a walk and a swim. Cove East is a California Tahoe Conservancy Restoration Project, so dogs must be leashed so they don't disturb the wildlife. Follow the sandy path which will take you along the opening of the Truckee River to a small grassy beach. From the South Lake Tahoe Y, drive east on Hwy 50 for approximately 0.5 miles and turn left on Tahoe Keys Blvd. Just before you enter the Tahoe Keys, turn right on Venice Dr. and follow to the end of the road, where you will see Cove East off to the right. Park along the street and walk between the 2 chain link fences. Follow the path to the lake.

Kiva Beach
This sandy beach has restrooms and picnic tables. Dogs must be leashed. From South Lake Tahoe Y, drive north on Hwy 89 for 2.5 miles to Kiva Beach.

Echo Lakes

This is a great spot for you and your dog to picnic and swim. There is a water taxi that can take both of you across the lake. From South Lake Tahoe Y, drive south on Hwy 50 for 9.6 miles and turn right on Echo Lakes Road. Continue to an intersection and turn left. Park in the upper lot at the Echo Lakes Resort. The water taxi leaves from the boat dock at the Echo Lakes Resort. The water taxi usually runs between Memorial Day and Labor Day, from 8 am to 5 pm. $6 per person, $3 per dog. For more information, call (530) 659-7207.

Fallen Leaf Lake

This scenic lake is a great spot for picnicking, swimming, fishing, camping and biking. From the South Lake Tahoe Y, drive north on Hwy 89 and turn left on Fallen Leaf Lake Road. Follow the road to the lake.

Gus, Boxer/Husky mix

Lake Tahoe Nevada State Park - Cave Rock

This state park is really nothing more than a parking lot surrounded with water. One side of the lot is sandy, which dogs are not allowed on. The other 3 sides are rocky, but dogs are free to swim their heart's content. Dogs can also play on the rocky peninsula, just past the sandy beach. There is a boat ramp which dogs are allowed to play on, as long as there are no boats around. We found this spot very useful when we had 3 muddy dogs and just needed a place to rinse them off. From the casinos (Stateline) drive north on Hwy 50 for 6.7 miles and turn left into the parking lot. $5/day or $2 for 15 minutes. Dogs must be on leash.

Tallac Historic Site

Leashed dogs are allowed on the grounds and at the beach of the Tallac Historic Site. While you are there, check out the three historic estates: Pope, Valhalla, and Baldwin. From South Lake Tahoe Y, drive north on Hwy 89 for approximately 3 miles and turn right at the sign for the Tallac Historic Site.

To be without a dog is worse than to be without a song.

–Henry Beetle Hough

FISHING SPOTS

Bogey, Black Lab

TRUCKEE

Truckee River in Glenshire

The fishing is great in the Truckee River. Catch and release only in this area. From Truckee, drive east on Donner Pass Road, past downtown and turn right on Glenshire Drive. Go 4.5 miles and turn right just past Glenshire Bridge. Follow the dirt road and park near the river.

Martis Creek Lake

This lake is a popular spot for fly fishing and only allows catch and release. It's known for its Lahonton cutthroat trout, German brown trout, and Eagle Lake-strain rainbow trout. Artificial lures and flies with barbless hooks only. From Truckee, drive south on Hwy 267 for 6 miles. Turn left at the Martis Creek Lake sign, and drive 0.5 miles to the lake.

Boca Reservoir

This large reservoir is stocked with kokanee salmon, rainbow trout and brown trout. From Truckee, drive 7 miles east on I-80 and take the Hirschdale Exit. Drive north on Stampede Dam Road to the lake.

Stampede Reservoir

This popular fishing spot is filled with kokanee salmon, mountain whitefish, rainbow trout, Mackinaw trout, brook trout and brown trout. From Truckee, drive 7 miles east on I-80 to the Hirschdale Exit. Drive north on Stampede Dam Road for 8 miles to the Stampede Reservoir.

Prosser Creek Reservoir

Rainbow and brown trout inhabit this lake. Trolling is good along the shore. From Truckee, drive north on Hwy 89 for 2.5 miles and turn right on Prosser Dam Road.

Sagehen Creek

You'll be likely to catch rainbow, brook or brown trout in this creek. Catch and release only in this area. From Truckee, drive north on Hwy 89 for 7.5 miles to where the creek crosses under the highway.

WEST SHORE

Desolation Wilderness Lakes
There are numerous lakes in the Desolation Wilderness area that have great fishing. You will need to hike in to get to the lakes. Check out the Hiking Trails section of this book for trail directions to get to these great fishing spots: Velma Lakes, Granite Lake, Crag Lake, and Susie Lake.

INCLINE VILLAGE

Spooner Lake
This small lake is filled with cutthroat trout. Catch and release only. From Incline Village, drive south on Hwy 28 approximately 9 miles to Spooner Lake at the Nevada State Park.

SOUTH LAKE TAHOE

Fallen Leaf Lake
There is an abundant supply kokanee salmon and Mackinaw trout in this large lake. From the South Lake Tahoe Y, drive north on Hwy 89 and turn left on Fallen Leaf Lake Road.

Taylor Creek
Fallen Leaf Lake releases water periodically into Taylor Creek. Along with kokanee salmon, the creek is filled with rainbow and brown trout. From South Lake Tahoe Y, drive north on Hwy 89 for 3.2 miles to the Taylor Creek Visitors Center. Park and walk towards the creek.

Echo Lakes
Upper and Lower Echo Lakes are connected by a small channel. Both are filled with kokanee salmon, cutthroat trout, rainbow trout and brook trout. From South Lake Tahoe Y, drive south on Hwy 50 for 9.6 miles and turn right on Echo Lakes Road. Continue to an intersection and turn left. Park in the upper lot at the Echo Lakes Resort.

*A dog is the one thing on earth that loves
you more than you love yourself.*

–Josh Billings

OTHER DOGGIE ADVENTURES

Tucker, Golden Retriever

TRUCKEE

Dairy Queen Puppy Cup

Drive through the Dairy Queen in Truckee, and receive a free 'puppy cup' of vanilla ice cream for your dog. 11355 Donner Pass Road, Donner Plaza, Truckee (530) 587-7055.

NORTH SHORE

Squaw Valley Tram Ride

During the summer months, you and your dog can take the tram to the top of Squaw Valley. At the top, you will find fields of wildflowers and many trails to explore. Dogs must be leashed on the tram. The tram costs $16 for adults, and after 5pm, it's $7. Dogs are free. For more information, call (530) 583-6985.

Rafting Down the Truckee

What could be better than a relaxing summer day, rafting down the Truckee River with your dog. Raft rentals are available at Mountain Air Sports, located at 205 River Road, along Hwy 89 and Fanny Bridge Raft Rentals, located near Fanny Bridge. Only some dogs are allowed, depending on their size and the sharpness of their claws. You may want to call first. Mountain Air Sports (530) 583-5606, Fanny Bridge Raft Rentals (530) 583-0123.

Fishing Charters and Lake Tours

The six hour fishing charters go out in the morning and afternoon, and run $65 per person. Tackle is supplied. Lake tours are $70 per hour and include a BBQ lunch on the boat. Two dogs allowed on the boat. For more information, contact Pete at The Reel Deal Sportfishing & Lake Tours (530) 581-0924, or (530) 206-REEL.

Double Dawg Jawg

This annual fund raiser is held by the Naughty Dawg Saloon and Grill in Tahoe City. It benefits the needy animals at the Pet Network of Lake Tahoe. The 2 mile jog starts at the Naughty Dawg and loops behind the Tahoe City Golf Course. This loop can be done twice if desired. A $15 fee gets you and your dog into the race, and gets you a t-shirt. After, there is a raffle with great prizes from local sponsors. For more information, call the Naughty Dawg at (530) 583-DAWG.

Naughty Dawg Monster Dog Pull

The Naughty Dawg Saloon & Grill puts on this contest annually in Tahoe City as part of Snowfest, usually the end of February. The dogs are harnessed to one of several different sizes of beer kegs, depending on their weight. The first dog to pull the keg of beer over the finish line wins. All dogs that enter receive prizes. $5 to enter your dog. The contest benefits the Pet Network of Lake Tahoe. For more information, call The Naughty Dawg at (530) 581-DAWG or Snowfest at (530) 583-7625.

Dress Up Your Dog Contest

This contest is put on by the Agate Bay Animal Hospital annually in North Lake Tahoe during Snowfest, usually the end of February. The categories include: Cutest, Looks Most Like Owner, Best Group Act, Most Original, and Looks Most Like Famous Person. Prizes are given to all who enter. $5 to enter your dog. For more information, call the Agate Bay Animal Hospital at (530) 546-7522 or Snowfest at (530) 583-7625.

Tahoe Cross Country Season Pass for Dogs

Now you can cross country ski with your pooch on groomed trails! There are 2 trails open to dogs, which are allowed leash-free but under voice control. Doggie bags are provided for cleaning up messes. Dogs are allowed Mon - Fri 8:30am - 5:00pm and Saturday, Sunday and Holidays 2:00pm - 5:00pm. A season pass is $45 for 1 dog and $75 for 2 dogs. Day passes are also available at $3 per day per dog. For more information, call (530) 583.5475. Located at 925 Country Club Dr., Tahoe City.

Wedding Bells

You can't get married without your best friend! A Chapel by the River, can accommodate your desire to have your furry friend present on your wedding day. 115 West Lake Blvd, Tahoe City (530) 581-2757.

WEST SHORE

Emerald Bay Boat-In Camp

One of the most popular campsites around, this spot is complete with a large pier and a long sandy beach. Check out Vikingsholm during the day, and camp here at night. Dogs must be leashed and are not allowed in Vikingsholm. Closed for the winter. 20 sites, $10 fee. Located on the north side of Emerald Bay. For more information, call (530) 525-7277.

Mountain High Weddings

Looking to get married atop a mountain overlooking the lake? Mountain High Weddings holds ceremonies on the north and west shores of the lake, and your pooch is more than welcome to attend. For more information, call (530) 525-9320.

Maggie, Yellow Lab

INCLINE VILLAGE

Annual Pet Walk

This fund raiser is held by the Pet Network of Lake Tahoe every summer in Incline Village. It benefits needy pets and helps find them new homes. There are food booths, crafts, dog contests and demonstrations. A $10 entrance fee gets you a Pet Network t-shirt, and gets your dog a bandana and a bag of treats. For more information, call the Pet Network at (775) 832-4404.

SOUTH LAKE TAHOE

Echo Lakes Boat Tour

Over summer you and your dog can get a guided tour of Echo Lakes. This 1.5 hour tour is complete with a Forest Service Naturalist, ready to tell you and your dog all that you ever wanted to know about this spectacular area. The tours are Thursday mornings at 10:00 am. The boat acts as a water taxi the rest of the day, bringing hikers back and forth across the 2.5 mile lake. The water taxi hours are 8 am to 6 pm. The boat usually runs between Memorial Day and Labor Day, depending on the weather. From South Lake Tahoe Y, drive south on Hwy 50 for 9.6 miles and turn right on Echo Lakes Road. Continue to an intersection and turn left. Park in the upper lot at the Echo Lakes Resort. The boat tour and water taxi leaves from the boat dock at the Echo Lakes Resort. For more information, call (530) 659-7207.

Sorensen's Resort

This resort offers lodging as well as many activities for adults, kids and dogs. It is located on 165 acres, where your dog can run leash-free. The resort offers educational programs, including history tours, birdwatching, fly-fishing workshops, nature photography, medicine in the mountains, wildflower tours, guided hikes, and arts and crafts. They also have other activities nearby, including horseback riding, snowshoeing, hiking, mountain biking, kayaking and white water rafting. Located in Hope Valley, which is about 20 miles south of Lake Tahoe and 15 minutes from Kirkwood Ski Resort. 14255 Hwy 88, Hope Valley (530) 694-2203 or (800) 423-9949 Website: www.sorensensresort.com E-mail: sorensensresort@yahoo.com

Taylor Creek Visitors Center

Come see Mother Nature at her finest. There are guided nature trails, daily discussion groups about different aspects of Lake Tahoe, even a campfire program with discussions, songs and marshmallows. And your well-behaved dog is allowed at all of them. There is a lot to explore here, including an underground stream profile chamber. Dogs must be leashed. From South Lake Tahoe Y, drive north on Hwy 89 for 3.5 miles at turn right into the Visitors Center. For more information about activities and program schedules, call (530) 573-2600 or (530) 573-2694.

Kokanee Salmon Festival

This 2 day festival is held annually in October at the Taylor Creek Visitors Center to celebrate the spawning of the Kokanee Salmon. There are special events, great food and music, fun contests, and interpretive programs. Grab the kids and the dog and make a day of it! For more information, call (530) 573-2600.

Timber, Springer Spaniel

Sportfishing Charters

Your dog will love feeling the wind through his hair as you set out for a day of fishing in Lake Tahoe. These 1/2 day or full day trips run year round, with all of the fishing gear furnished. Captain Dean and Captain John can accommodate any size party, with their 7 fishing boats. Located in the Ski Run Marina. For more information, call (530) 541-5448 or (800) 696-7797.

Tahoe Keys Boat Rentals

Now you can cruise the lake with your furry friend! Just make sure you clean up any messes your pooch may leave behind. Boat rentals are seasonal. Located at the end of Venice Drive in the Tahoe Keys. (530) 544-8888.

Wedding Bells

You can't walk down the aisle without your best friend at your side! The Chapel of the Bells is happy to have your furry friend join you on this joyous day. 2700 Lake Tahoe Blvd, South Lake Tahoe (800) 247-4333 or (530) 544-1112.

Camp Winnaribbun

This unique vacation camp has usually three 1-week long sessions every summer. Dogs and their owners are invited to stay at cabins right by the beach and participate in numerous activities, including, hiking, canoeing, agility, carting, tracking and herding. They also have programs such as search and rescue, pet therapy, and homeopathic medicine. The days end with gourmet meals and campfire entertainment. The camps book up fast, so call early to register. (775) 348-8412
Website: www.campw.com
E-mail: info@campw.com

To err is human, to forgive, canine.

-Unknown

DOGGIE
SERVICES

Pozo, Pit Bull Mix

PET SHOPS

TRUCKEE

Gateway Pets
Gateway Shopping Center, 1120 Donner Pass Road, Truckee
(530) 582-0608

Mickey's Pet Shop
Westgate Shopping Center, 11429 Donner Pass Road, Truckee
(530) 587-1675

NORTH SHORE

C&C Pet Stop
950 North Lake Blvd, Tahoe City (530) 581-4828

INCLINE VILLAGE

Incline Royal Pet Boutique & Salon
Regal Bone Bakery
760 Mays Blvd, Suite #4, Incline Village (775) 831-4694

SOUTH LAKE TAHOE

Animal Works
2291 Lake Tahoe Blvd, SLK Tahoe (530) 541-3831

Pet Supermarket
1074 Emerald Bay Road, SLK Tahoe (530) 544-9133

Zephyr Feed & Boarding
396 Dorla Ct., Zephyr Cove (775) 588-3907

VETERINARIANS

TRUCKEE

Donner-Truckee Veterinary Hospital
9701 North Shore Blvd, Truckee (530) 587-4366

Sierra Pet Clinic of Truckee
10411 River Park Place, Truckee (530) 587-7200

NORTH SHORE

North Lake Veterinary Clinic
2933 Lake Forest Rd, Tahoe City (530) 583-8587

Agate Bay Animal Hospital
8428 Trout Ave, Kings Beach (530) 546-7522

INCLINE VILLAGE

Incline Veterinary Hospital
880 Tanager, Incline Village (775) 831-0433

SOUTH LAKE TAHOE

Alpine Animal Hospital
921 Emerald Bay Rd, SLK Tahoe (530) 541-4040

Alpine-Round Hill Animal Hospital
392 Dorla Ct, Elk Point (775) 588-8744

Emerald Bay Veterinary Hospital
1022 Emerald Bay Road, SLK Tahoe (530) 544-2518

Kingsbury Veterinary Hospital
183 Shady Ln, Stateline (775) 588-3828

Sierra Veterinary Hospital
3095 Hwy 50, SLK Tahoe (530) 542-1952

South Tahoe Veterinary Hospital
964 Rubicon Tr, SLK Tahoe (530) 541-3551

DOG GROOMERS

TRUCKEE

Gateway Pets
Gateway Shopping Center, 11200 Donner Pass Road,
Truckee (530) 582-0608

Mickey's Launder-Mutt
Westgate Shopping Center, 11429 Donner Pass Road,
Truckee (530) 587-0366

Sierra Pet Clinic of Truckee
10411 River Park Place, Truckee (530) 587-7200

NORTH SHORE

Jo-Mar's Pet Coiffures
8775 North Lake Blvd, Kings Beach (530) 546-5756

North Lake Pet Grooming
2993 Lake Forest Road, Tahoe City (530) 581-5466

INCLINE VILLAGE

Incline Royal Pet Boutique & Salon
760 Mays Blvd, Suite #4, Incline Village (775) 831-4694

SOUTH LAKE TAHOE

The Dog House and Cattery
260 Kingsbury Grade, Kingsbury (775) 588-4621

Four Paws Grooming & Boarding
979 Tallac Ave, SLK Tahoe (530) 542-2377

Jacki Wright's Mobile Dog & Cat Grooming
Mobile Dog and Cat Salon (530) 542-1777

Paw Spa
2494 Lake Tahoe Blvd, A-7 Pine Cone Plaza
(530) 544-PAWS

Posh Paws
Mobile Dog Salon (775) 588-PAWS

DOG KENNELS

TRUCKEE

Bed & Breakfast For Pets
Highway 267, Truckee (530) 587-3596

Truckee-Sierra Boarding Kennel
Hwy 89 & Alder Creek Road, Truckee (530) 587-2678

NORTH SHORE

Agate Bay Animal Hospital
8428 Trout Ave, Kings Beach (530) 546-7522

North Lake Veterinary Clinic
2933 Lake Forest Road, Tahoe City (530) 583-8587

INCLINE VILLAGE

Pet Network Boarding & Day Care
401 Village Blvd, (775) 833-0273

Incline Veterinary Hospital
880 Tanager, Incline Village (775) 831-0433

SOUTH LAKE TAHOE

Alpine Animal Hospital
921 Emerald Bay Rd, SLK Tahoe (530) 541-4040

Four Paws Grooming and Boarding
979 Tallac Ave, SLK Tahoe (530) 542-2377

Sierra Veterinary Hospital
3095 Hwy 50, SLK Tahoe (530) 542-1952

South Tahoe Veterinary Hospital
964 Rubicon Tr, SLK Tahoe (530) 541-3551

Zephyr Feed and Boarding
396 Dorla Ct., Zephyr Cove (775) 588-3907

DOG SITTERS

TRUCKEE

High Sierra Professional Pet Sitting
(530) 583-8999

Pampered Pet Care
Marjie Aubrey (530) 587-2701

Truckee Tails
(530) 582-6964

NORTH SHORE

Doggie Day Care & Overnight Boarding
Sue Kirk (530) 583-9537

Doggie Love Day Care
Lisa (530) 525-6189
www.doggielovedaycare.com
doggielovedaycare@tahoe.com

High Sierra Professional Pet Sitting
(530) 583-8999

North Lake Pet Sitters
(530) 320-5662

Walking The Dog
(530) 583-DOGS

INCLINE VILLAGE

Pet Network Boarding & Day Care
401 Village Blvd., (775) 833-0273

SOUTH LAKE TAHOE

A Tender Loving Care
South Lake Tahoe, (530) 541-5197

Happy Tails of Tahoe
South Lake Tahoe, (530) 573-0220

Paw Prints
South Lake Tahoe, (530) 577-4618

DOG TRAINERS

Beyond Obedience
Jeanie Collins (530) 587-4499 Truckee
Canine Behavioral Consultant

Guy Yeaman- Professional Dog Trainer
(775) 265-4530 North Shore, South Shore

The Dog Trainer
Sandra Hann (530) 546-0966 North Shore

DOG FENCING

Invisible Fencing of Sierra
Truckee, (800) 727-1411

Dog Watch
Truckee, (530) 582-5558

Alpine Fence Company
848 Tanager Bldg. G, Incline Village (775) 831-6231
Dog Runs, Dog Kennels

Tahoe Fence Company
South Lake Tahoe, (800) 332-2822
Dog Runs, Dog Kennels

South Shore Fence
1640 Apache Dr, South Lake Tahoe (530) 573-8923
Dog Runs, Dog Kennels

Lake Tahoe Dog Laws

In and around Lake Tahoe, Leash Laws require you to have your dog on leash and under voice control. A dog is 'at large' when he is under no supervision, without a leash or restraint and on someone else's property. Dogs will be picked up by an animal control officer when they are 'at large' and taken to a nearby animal shelter.

Truckee has a Control Law, which allows the dog to be off leash, but under visual and voice control. A dog will be picked up in this area for being 'at large' when he is unsupervised and on someone else's property.

Sno-Park Permits

Sno-Park permits are required for parking at designated Sno-Park areas. A day permit is $5 and a season permit is $25. Permits are available at the following locations:

Truckee:
Emigrant Trail Museum, Donner Memorial State Park
(530) 587-3841

North Shore:
Alpenglow Sports, 415 North Lake Blvd, Tahoe City
(530) 583-6917

AAA (Members) 7717 North Lake Blvd, Kings Beach
(530) 546-4245

West Shore:
Homewood Hardware, 5405 West Lake Blvd, Homewood
(530) 525-6367

South Shore:
AAA (Members) 961 Emerald Bay Road, SLK Tahoe
(530) 541-4434

South Tahoe Shell, 1020 Emerald Bay Rd, SLK Tahoe
(530) 541-2720

Meyers Shell and Food Mart, 2950 Hwy 50, Meyers
(530) 577-4533

Wilderness Permits

Wilderness permits are required when hiking or camping in
Desolation Wilderness. There are two different permits, one for
day users and one for overnight camping.

Day Use Permits
The day use permit is free and is available with self-registra-
tion, at most of the trailheads into Desolation Wilderness. They
are also available at the Lake Tahoe Basin Management Office
at 870 Emerald Bay Road, Suite #1, SLK Tahoe (530) 573-2600.

Overnight Use Permits
Those who plan to spend the night in Desolation Wilderness
must register at the Lake Tahoe Basin Management Office in
South Lake Tahoe. There is a quota system in effect to limit the
number of overnight users in Desolation Wilderness. One
permit is good for up to 15 people, and 700 permits is the limit
per day. Half of the permits available can be reserved up to 90
days in advance, and the rest are issued that day on a first
come, first serve basis. Open campfires are not allowed in
Desolation Wilderness, use only portable gas stoves. For more
information, contact the Lake Tahoe Basin Management Office
at 870 Emerald bay Rd, Suite #1, SLK Tahoe, (530) 573-2600.

TAHOE DOG TIPS

WINTER TIPS

If your dog gets dry, itchy skin from the cold winter air, add a teaspoon of canola oil daily to their food. You will start seeing an improvement in your dog's coat in a few weeks.

Make sure to comb your dog's thick coat over winter. Dirt can get trapped against the skin and cause your dog to have skin irritations or skin diseases.

To remove mats from your dog's fir, sprinkle cornstarch on the mat, and the tangle should come right out.

During the winter, be aware that salting your icy driveway can burn the pads on your dog's feet.

Keep your dog from getting frost-bitten feet by keeping the hair in between his toes trimmed. This will prevent snow from accumulating between his toes and causing frostbite.

Some people will put anti freeze in their toilets over winter to keep the pipes from freezing. Be aware of this when bringing your dog into someone else's home.

During winter, dogs use up more energy keeping warm. Remember this during feeding time, a little extra food will help.

TAHOE DOG TIPS

SUMMER TIPS

Don't give your long haired dog a haircut over summer. That thick coat can actually keep him cooler.

To remove sap from your dog's fur, try either mayonnaise or Avon Skin-So-Soft lotion.

Take your dog out for his walk in the morning or evening to avoid the heat.

Get a small wading pool and fill it with water. Your dog will enjoy cooling off on hot summer days.

Dogs will double their water intake during the hot summer months. Leave out an extra bowl of water out for them during this time.

Never leave your dog alone in a car during the summer. It only takes a few minutes for the temperature in your car to increase dramatically, which can be life-threatening to your dog.

Dogs can get sunburns and skin cancer. If your dog's in the sun most of the day, consider putting an SPF sunscreen on his nose and ears. Avoid sunscreens that contain zinc, they can be harmful to your dog if swallowed.

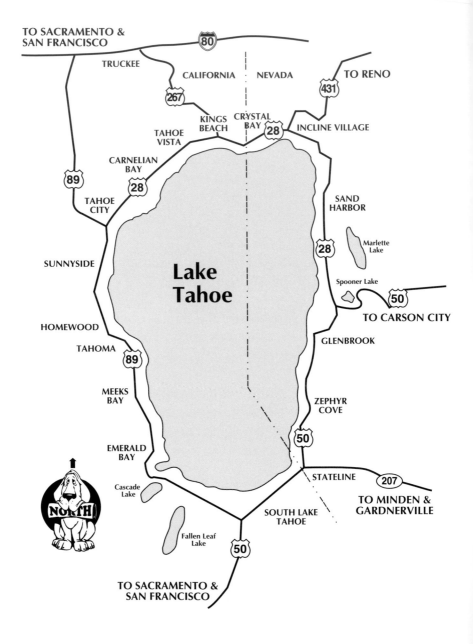

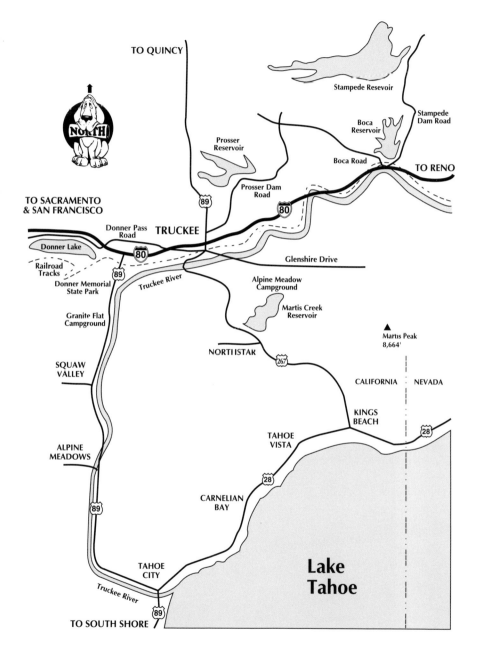

TO QUINCY

Stampede Resevoir

Stampede Dam Road

Boca Reservoir

Prosser Reservoir

Boca Road

TO RENO

Prosser Dam Road

89

80

TO SACRAMENTO & SAN FRANCISCO

Donner Pass Road

TRUCKEE

Glenshire Drive

Donner Lake

80

Railroad Tracks

89

Truckee River

Donner Memorial State Park

Alpine Meadow Campground

Martis Creek Reservoir

Granite Flat Campground

Martis Peak 8,664'

NORTHSTAR

267

SQUAW VALLEY

CALIFORNIA   NEVADA

KINGS BEACH

ALPINE MEADOWS

TAHOE VISTA

28

28

89

CARNELIAN BAY

Lake Tahoe

TAHOE CITY

Truckee River

89

TO SOUTH SHORE

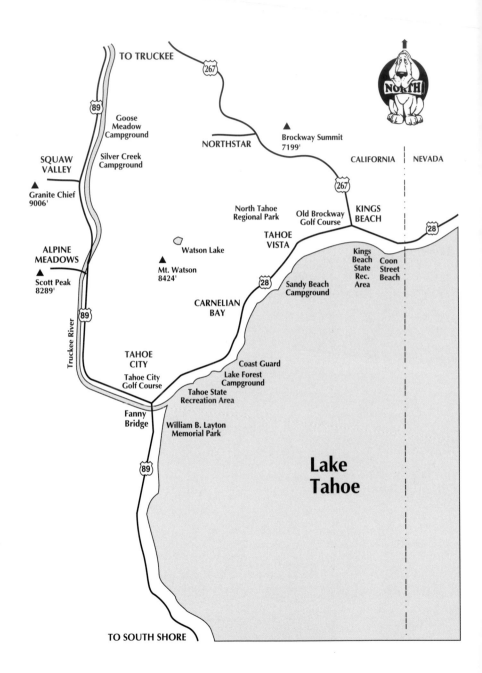

TO TRUCKEE

267

89

Goose
Meadow
Campground

NORTHSTAR

Brockway Summit
7199'

CALIFORNIA | NEVADA

SQUAW
VALLEY

Silver Creek
Campground

267

Granite Chief
9006'

North Tahoe
Regional Park

Old Brockway
Golf Course

KINGS
BEACH

28

TAHOE
VISTA

ALPINE
MEADOWS

Watson Lake

Kings
Beach
State
Rec.
Area

Coon
Street
Beach

Mt. Watson
8424'

Scott Peak
8289'

28

Sandy Beach
Campground

89

CARNELIAN
BAY

Truckee River

TAHOE
CITY

Coast Guard
Lake Forest
Campground

Tahoe City
Golf Course

Tahoe State
Recreation Area

Fanny
Bridge

William B. Layton
Memorial Park

89

Lake
Tahoe

TO SOUTH SHORE

120

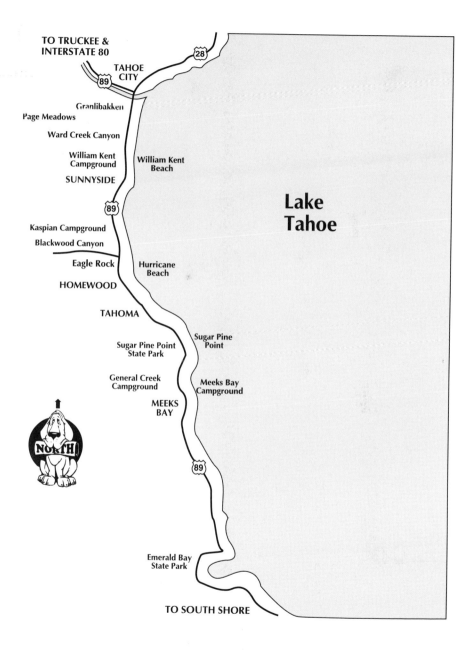

TO TRUCKEE &
INTERSTATE 80

28

89

TAHOE
CITY

Granlibakken

Page Meadows

Ward Creek Canyon

William Kent
Campground

William Kent
Beach

SUNNYSIDE

89

Kaspian Campground

Blackwood Canyon

Eagle Rock

Hurricane
Beach

HOMEWOOD

TAHOMA

Sugar Pine
Point

Sugar Pine Point
State Park

General Creek
Campground

Meeks Bay
Campground

MEEKS
BAY

**Lake
Tahoe**

89

NORTH

Emerald Bay
State Park

TO SOUTH SHORE

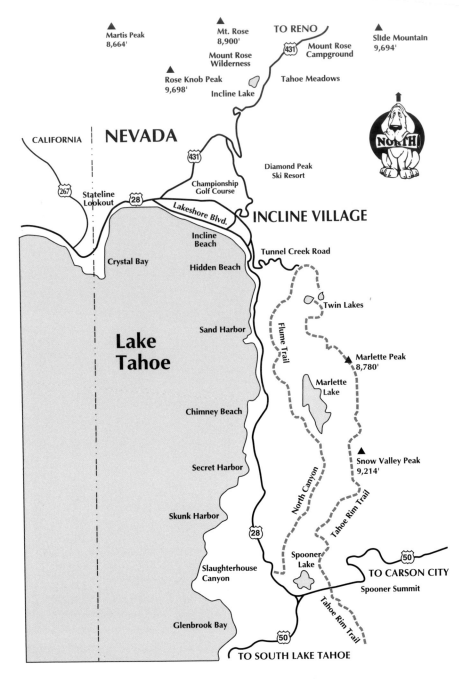

Martis Peak
8,664'

Mt. Rose
8,900'

TO RENO

431

Mount Rose
Wilderness

Mount Rose
Campground

Slide Mountain
9,694'

Rose Knob Peak
9,698'

Tahoe Meadows

Incline Lake

CALIFORNIA | NEVADA

431

Diamond Peak
Ski Resort

267

Stateline
Lookout

28

Championship
Golf Course

Lakeshore Blvd.

INCLINE VILLAGE

Incline
Beach

Tunnel Creek Road

Crystal Bay

Hidden Beach

Twin Lakes

Lake
Tahoe

Sand Harbor

Flume Trail

Marlette Peak
8,780'

Marlette
Lake

Chimney Beach

Snow Valley Peak
9,214'

Secret Harbor

North Canyon

Tahoe Rim Trail

Skunk Harbor

28

Spooner
Lake

50

TO CARSON CITY

Slaughterhouse
Canyon

Spooner Summit

Glenbrook Bay

50

Tahoe Rim Trail

TO SOUTH LAKE TAHOE

122

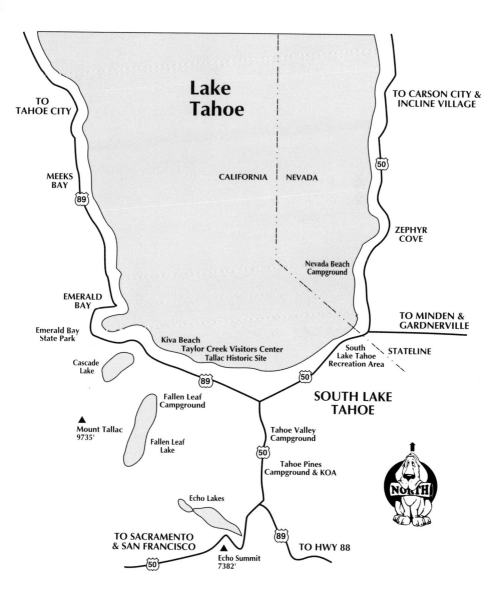

Lake Tahoe

TO TAHOE CITY

TO CARSON CITY & INCLINE VILLAGE

50

MEEKS BAY

89

CALIFORNIA | NEVADA

ZEPHYR COVE

EMERALD BAY

Nevada Beach Campground

Emerald Bay State Park

TO MINDEN & GARDNERVILLE

Cascade Lake

Kiva Beach
Taylor Creek Visitors Center
Tallac Historic Site

South Lake Tahoe Recreation Area

STATELINE

89

50

SOUTH LAKE TAHOE

▲ Mount Tallac 9735'

Fallen Leaf Campground

Fallen Leaf Lake

Tahoe Valley Campground

50

Tahoe Pines Campground & KOA

Echo Lakes

TO SACRAMENTO & SAN FRANCISCO

50

▲ Echo Summit 7382'

89

TO HWY 88

Dog Haiku

I love my master;
Thus I perfume myself with
This long-rotten squirrel.

I lie belly-up in the sunshine,
Happier than you will ever be.

Today I sniffed many dog butts-
I celebrate by kissing your face.

I sound the alarm!
Paperboy- come to kill us all-
Look! Look! Look! Look! Look!

I sound the alarm!
Mailman Fiend- come to kill us all-
Look! Look! Look! Look! Look!

I sound the alarm!
Meter reader- come to kill all-
Look! Look! Look! Look! Look!

I sound the alarm!
Garbage man- come to kill us all-
Look! Look! Look! Look! Look!

I sound the alarm!
Neighbor's cat- dares to enter yard!
Look! Look! Look! Look! Look!

I lift my leg and wiz on each bush.
Hello, Spot - sniff this and weep.

How do I love thee?
The ways are as numberless as
My hairs on the rug.

My human is home!
I am so ecstatic I have
Made a puddle.

I hate my choke chain -
Look, world, they strangle me!
Ack Ack Ack Ack Ack Ack!

Sleeping here, my chin
On your foot - no greater bliss -
Well, maybe chasing cats...

Look in my eyes and deny it.
No human could love you
As much I do.

The cat is not all bad-
She fills the litter box
With Tootsie Rolls.

Dig under fence-why?
Because it's there. Because it's there.
Because it's there.

I am your best friend,
Now, always, and especially
When you are eating.

You may call them fleas,
But they are far more -
I call them a vocation.

My owners' mood is romantic-
I lie near their feet.
I fart a big one.

Author Unknown

The Rescue Dog

I took a little dog home that day,
He was ugly and bad, it's true,
Only I could see
His true beauty shining through.

I put him down at my front door,
So he could walk inside,
And when I opened up for him,
He just stood there, eyes open wide.

A big soft bed was there for him,
A fluffy blanket blue,
A heap of toys was nearby,
All bright and shiny new.

All this for me, he seemed to say,
His little eyes they shone,
No more need to bite, or cower or cringe
All fear and anger gone.

He paid me back a thousand times
My furry faithful friend,
A better friend I never had
Right up until the end.

We walked a long and rocky road,
Through trouble, grief and strife,
And in the dark and stormy days
He gave meaning to my life.

I thought my heart would break
When the time came for him to go,
I buried him in his blanket blue
Beneath the cold white snow.

Sometimes I still hear his little bark,
Feel the touch of a velvet paw,
And I still stoop down to greet him
When I open my front door.

Author Unknown

Behind This Kennel Door

As a pup I dreamed and wondered
What life would hold in store.
For me, I thought, there's something great
Beyond this kennel door.

Out there are needy people
And I have much to give:
Love, and wit, and gentleness
To help them learn and live.

I'd be someone's protector,
Keep little ones from harm,
Or guide an old man's weary steps,
Or help to run a farm.

I'd run and bark and jump and play
With friends along a sandy shore.
I'd roll in meadows thick and green
That lie behind this kennel door.

I'd lay there waiting -- longing --
As the days and years went by.
My owner kept me fed and brushed,
But inside, he let me die.

I do not think of greatness now.
I'm old and filled with pain,
My owner has some ribbons,
But I have lived in vain.

I cannot think what could have been,
My dreams are filled with hope no more,
Just floor and walls and broken heart
Behind this kennel door.

Author Unknown

If It Should Be

If it should be I grow frail and weak
And pain prevents my peaceful sleep.
Then you must do what must be done
When this last battle can't be won.

You will be sad, I understand.
But don't let grief then stay your hand
For on this day, more than the rest
Your love and friendship must stand the test.

We've had so many happy years
That what's to come can hold no fears
You'd not want me to suffer so
When the time comes, please let me go.

Take me where my needs they'll tend
Only, stay with me until the end.
Hold me firm and speak to me.
Until my eyes no longer see.

I know, in time, you, too will see
It is kindness that you do for me
Although my tail its last has waved
From pain and suffering I've been saved.

Do not grieve it should be you
Who must decide this thing to do
We've been so close, we two, these years
Don't let your heart hold any tears.

Anonymous

INDEX

THE DOG LOVER'S GUIDE TO LAKE TAHOE

THE END

NOTES

NOTES